**NEW DIRECTIONS
FOR CONTINUING
EDUCATION**

Number 4 • 1979

NEW DIRECTIONS FOR CONTINUING EDUCATION

A Quarterly Sourcebook
Alan B. Knox, Editor-in-Chief

Number 4, 1979

Attracting Able Instructors of Adults

M. Alan Brown
Harlan G. Copeland
Guest Editors

Jossey-Bass Inc., Publishers
San Francisco • Washington • London

LC
5219
.A89

ATTRACTING ABLE INSTRUCTORS OF ADULTS
New Directions for Continuing Education
Number 4, 1979
    M. Alan Brown, Harlan G. Copeland, Guest Editors

Copyright © 1979 by Jossey-Bass Inc., Publishers
                   and
               Jossey-Bass Limited

Copyright under International, Pan American, and Universal Copyright Conventions. All rights reserved. No part of this issue may be reproduced in any form—except for brief quotation (not to exceed 500 words) in a review or professional work—without permission in writing from the publishers.

New Directions for Continuing Education (publication number 0195-2242) quarterly by Jossey-Bass Inc., Publishers. Subscriptions are available at the regular rate for institutions, libraries, and agencies of $25 for one year. Individuals may subscribe at the special professional rate of $15 for one year.

Correspondence:
Subscriptions, single-issue orders, change of address notices, undelivered copies, and other correspondence should be sent to *New Directions* Subscriptions, Jossey-Bass Inc., Publishers, 433 California Street, San Francisco, California 94104. Editorial correspondence should be sent to the Editor-in-Chief, Alan B. Knox, Office for the Study of Continuing Professional Education, University of Illinois at Urbanaffl Champaign, Urbana, Illinois 61801.

Library of Congress Catalogue Card Number LC 79-89389

Cover design by Willi Baum
Manufactured in the United States of America

Contents

Editors' Notes: Perspectives on a Staffing Strategy   *M. Alan Brown, Harlan G. Copeland*   vii

Recruiting Teachers of Adults   *John H. Buskey*   1

Identifying a pool of qualified potential teachers is a critical first step in the staffing process; various techniques can be used to accomplish this. The development of a recruitment plan and a timetable for implementation are important to the success of the staffing process.

The Selection Process   *Gary J. Conti, Lee Porter*   15

When selecting from among many candidates, judgment must be based on the best information available. Is there a good match between job expectations and the proficiencies of the candidate? Securing useful information and the insight of a search committee will make the selection process more effective.

Staff Development: A Mandate for Organizational Survival   *Carroll A. Londoner*   25

A comprehensive program for staff development is an essential, ongoing process. The important elements in this process are involving teachers in planning the program, helping teachers understand the psychology of adult learning, and communicating the program goals, policies, and procedures of the organization to teachers.

Supervision and Monitoring   *Lloyd L. Brumfield, Doris P. Nesbit*   39

Supervising teachers of adults requires sensitivity and skill in order to achieve a relationship of openness and mutual trust. Such a relationship enables the administrator to help the teacher do the job that is expected.

Effective Administrative Support for Able Teachers   *Delight C. Willing*   51

The administrator has a continuing responsibility to provide the support that will allow able teachers to perform effectively. Satisfactory communications and a complete range of support services contribute to morale and effective teaching.

Developing a Comprehensive Reward System   *James C. Votruba*   59

Providing incentives for teachers of adults is an important means of attracting, retaining, and stimulating those who are able. A variety of extrinsic and intrinsic rewards and incentives are available to the administrator. Instituting these rewards appropriately and effectively is an important administrative function.

Learning as a Criterion of Success   Donald W. Mocker   71

Knowing who the able teachers are and assessing their effectiveness is an essential task but difficult to do well. Descriptions of three promising evaluation methods, along with an analysis of their advantages and disadvantages, provide a basis for developing an evaluation system that can be adapted to each situation.

New Directions for Attracting   Jerry Parsons   81
Able Teachers of Adults

The field of continuing education is undergoing dynamic change and challenge. To meet this challenge, administrators should develop strategies to employ the most creative and talented teachers available.

Supplementary Audiovisual   Darlene W. Elberling   89
Resources

A rich and diversified collection of audiovisual resources can be used by the administrator to enhance his or her proficiency in staffing.

Index   95

Editors' Notes: Perspectives on a Staffing Strategy

There are few areas of continuing education* practice more taken for granted than the staffing of teachers of adults. Consider how little attention this topic receives. When have consumer groups demanded that teachers of adults be licensed as a way of protecting learners from unqualified or unscrupulous practitioners? How often have labor unions tried to recruit part-time continuing education teachers? Typically, salaries for teachers of adults are grudgingly budgeted at minimum levels; in fact, volunteers are often preferred if they can be recruited. When salaries are paid, "overload" or part-time arrangements are desired because they do not require the additional costs of fringe benefits. Full-time contract positions for teachers of adults are scarce.

This sourcebook focuses on decisions regarding the staffing of teachers of adults. It is designed to help continuing education administrators improve their staffing practices. The authors have addressed from a program administrator's perspective the questions of teacher recruitment, selection, in-service education, supervision, rewards and recognition, evaluation, and administrative support, among others.

Many titles are used by those who select, develop, and supervise teachers of adults, including program administrator, conference coordinator, adult education administrator, continuing education administrator, and community education director. In this source book, the term *administrator* refers to all individuals who have responsibilities for employing and assisting persons who teach adults.

Focus on Teachers—A Needed Priority in Continuing Education

A vital task in all types of continuing education agencies is the acquisition of effective teachers. Careful program planning, magnificent facilities, and efficient administration are of no avail unless learning takes place. The bottom line in continuing education is that changes take place in the knowledge, skills, and attitudes of the adult participants in the program (be it course, meeting, workshop, lecture series, or broadcast).

Because instruction is central to the mission of continuing education, one might expect that the selection and development of teachers of adults would be a major and visible concern of the field. This does not seem to be the case. As the field has evolved, the full-time staff have been

---

*The term "continuing education" is used throughout this sourcebook to refer to all types of extension, adult, and continuing education programs.

administrators but not teachers. Houle's second category of adult educators—part-time leaders—includes most of those who teach in continuing education. Their part-time employment in continuing education is typically an addition to their other duties (Houle, 1960). For example, Park (1977) found that most adult basic education teachers (82 percent) are employed part-time.

This sourcebook on attracting and retaining able teachers of adults is timely. Since the public's expectations of continuing education have soared (Knox, 1979) and accountability has become a household word, it is essential that continuing educators use effective practices and policies in selecting and supporting teachers of adults.

A Staffing Strategy

The central concept in this sourcebook is that of a staffing strategy. An effective staffing strategy should apply, of course, to all staff members and volunteers in a continuing education agency. An effective staffing strategy for continuing education teachers is important because teachers are crucial to the success of the program and because their career path is so ill-defined. Strategy is an appropriate term because it implies that several different functions need to be performed and coordinated in such a way that successful teaching and learning will result. The plans for these coordinated functions constitute a staffing strategy.

The continuing education administrator has the overall responsibility for achieving maximum effectiveness in the teaching-learning process. To a large extent, the critical factor in achieving program excellence is the proficiency of the teaching staff. The teacher makes the class. A comprehensive staffing strategy can become the means for obtaining effective teaching. The success and satisfaction that adults derive from their learning experience are important indicators of program quality.

An effective staffing strategy can also produce a program that is rich and diverse in its offerings. A continuing education program is often built around the talents of the teachers, who are drawn from the community, as well as from the parent organization. Individuals with specialized and unique abilities need to be located or developed if the varied interests of adults are to be met.

Elements of a Staffing Strategy

The staffing strategy proposed here is based on the functions involved in finding, selecting, orienting, and rewarding those who teach in a continuing education program. Seven functions were identified: recruitment—the discovery and enlistment of people with the desired talent and abilities, selection—the act of choosing the person most likely to succeed as a teacher of adults in a specific program, providing administrative support—the provision of the support services and materials that facilitate the teaching-learning process, providing recognition—the provision of appropriate and meaningful rewards to teachers, staff development—the orientation and continuing education that enables teachers to improve their proficiency and performance, supervision—the provision of individual consultation and assistance by administrative personnel to improve the teaching-learning process, and evaluation—the appraisal of teacher performance for the purpose of improving it.

Teacher recruitment is the obvious first step in carrying out a staffing strategy. But, is it really so obvious? Are the expectations of the job defined? How extensive is the search? When does one begin? John Buskey explores these and other questions and suggests how a recruitment plan could be used.

An effective recruitment effort produces a number of qualified candidates. Gary Conti and Lee Porter discuss what is involved in the selection process. Various information gathering techniques such as reference checks and tests are discussed, and guidelines for interviewing candidates are presented.

Carroll Londoner proposes a staff development program consisting of both orientation and continuing education. What should the contents of such a program be? Who does the planning? Who provides the training? These and other questions confront the continuing education administrator.

Is there any need for the supervision of continuing education teachers? From the observations of many, there is very little actual supervision of teaching of adults in everyday practice. In college settings, some professors might regard supervision as interference with their academic freedom. In an adult basic education program the administrator might say, "I really don't know much about Ms. W's teaching. I haven't had a chance to observe her class." Unlike public school preparatory education or work in business and industry, where supervision is more visible, continuing education programs are often of short duration and nonrecurring. Lloyd Brumfield and Doris Nesbit make a case for supervision in continuing education. They stress, however, that successful supervision depends on the kind of relationship established between the administrator and the teacher. Several practical suggestions of ways supervisors can help teachers are offered by Brumfield and Nesbit.

Both Delight Willing and James Vortruba use Herzberg's (1966) motivators and personal hygiene factors theory to suggest ways administrators can understand and deal with the various motivations of teachers. Willing describes ways that administrative support can be provided to teachers. If this is lacking, dissatisfaction results. Vortruba, however, looks at ways administrators could provide meaningful rewards and incentives to teachers. These are "motivators" that result in satisfaction in a job.

An administrative function—teacher evaluation—is examined by Donald Mocker. This area has often been seen as impractical and inappropriate by administrators. The administrator who has to "break even" or "show a profit" has felt that he or she could not afford—either in money or time—systematic, objective evaluations. The numbers of enrollments became the most useful indicators for self-supporting programs and were used indirectly as measures of teaching effectiveness. Mocker reviews three techniques for evaluating teaching effectiveness and challenges us to make more use of learning as the criterion for teaching effectiveness.

As a summary, Jerry Parsons lists some new directions for attracting teachers of adults and implications of these directions for continuing education. He notes that this sourcebook can be a useful guide for the decade of the 1980s. If his suggestions for research are heeded, it is likely that the state of the art would be so advanced that a new sourcebook would be required in another ten years.

In the final chapter, Darlene Elberling provides suggestions for utilizing audiovisual resources in implementing a staffing strategy.

Although the role of the continuing education administrator is emphasized throughout this sourcebook, many individuals in the organization play a valuable and often crucial role in carrying through the ideas developed here. Leading and coordinating this total effort is the ongoing challenge and responsibility of the continuing education administrator.

References

Herzberg, F. and others. *Work and the Nature of Man.* New York: World, 1966.
Houle, C. O. "The Education of the Adult Educational Leaders." In M. S. Knowles (Ed.), *Handbook of Adult Education in the United States.* Chicago: Adult Education Association of the United States, 1960, p. 117-128.
Knox, A. B. "Overview, an Introduction to the Field." In A. B. Knox (Ed.), *Enhancing Proficiencies of Continuing Educators.* San Francisco: Jossey-Bass, 1979, p. 2.
Park, R. J. "Women in Adult Basic Education." *Lifelong Learning: The Adult Years,* December 1977, *1* (4), 12-13, 21.

M. Alan Brown is associate professor and director of the department of conferences at the University of Minnesota.

Harlan G. Copeland is associate professor with the graduate program in adult education at the University of Minnesota.

"The key to successful continuing education is good instruction, and good instructors are where you find them" (Sheldon and Wasinger, 1969, p. 280).

Recruiting Teachers of Adults

John H. Buskey

One of the most pressing concerns of continuing education program administrators is the acquisition, development, and retention of qualified teachers. How do administrators discover and recruit into their programs the most effective teachers? It is done, and done successfully, by administrators in a multitude of agencies, organizations, and institutions. After reviewing the literature on the topic of recruiting teachers for continuing education programs, however, one surmises that recruiting is one of those skills that is a genetic characteristic of continuing educators; no one talks about it—or even writes about it—and we are supposed to be able to do it because somehow, innately, we are born to it. In the literature one finds frequent reference to the selection of teachers and to the characteristics of effective teachers. But it would appear that we pluck them from the sky or that through some other mysterious process we gain access to a pool of talent from which we can select superior teachers who will become the stars of the program.

In recruiting teachers of adults, let us consider some questions that are central to the task. First, what kind of persons are we looking for? Where could we find them? How should we go about seeking them? When should we look for teachers? Can a plan for recruiting be developed that will, with some efficiency, provide a collection of well-qualified prospective teachers from which selections can be made?

The basic task of recruiting is to develop a pool of well-qualified applicants from which we can select those persons who can teach with a high degree of proficiency (Stanton, 1979). This process is systematic and continuous, but it must not absorb so much time that little else is accomplished. It is not a task best accomplished after the program has been scheduled and the students have enrolled.

There appear to be two basic approaches to staff recruitment, with numerous variations and nuances that make the task both interesting and complicated. The first, and probably the most common, is to identify a program (for example, an evening course, a correspondence course, a workshop, or a television course) and then seek an instructor capable of teaching it. This approach is common in situations where there is a standard curriculum, an existing set of instruction materials, or a specific task to be accomplished, as in a workshop. The second approach, normally a stroke of good luck, is to discover a person who is not only a good teacher but can also teach several courses. The task here is to discover the number of ways this person can contribute to the program.

Teachers of Adults

We are concerned here with all kinds of teachers of adults—those who teach in credit programs and those who teach in noncredit programs. Some will not be involved in direct institutional activities but will be creating and developing materials to be used by other teachers. Most will be part-time teachers of adults and will fit this form of teaching around another primary occupation, such as teaching high school or college students or managing a business or other career. A small minority will focus their full-time energies on teaching adult students.

Teachers of adults are recruited for a very wide range of instructional programs. The variety of roles for which instructors are needed for adult programs includes teachers in public school, college and university credit and noncredit evening programs; adult basic education teachers; trainers for human relations and management development seminars and workshops; volunteer leaders for church groups, the Cooperative Extension Service, or YWCA and YMCA programs; teachers for independent study by correspondence programs in colleges, universities, and proprietary schools; chairpersons for major research symposia and moderators for panel discussions at conferences; leaders for libraries' group discussion programs on current issues; instructors for college television courses; authors to write scripts and viewing notes for instructional television courses, syllabi for independent study by correspondence course, or handbooks for energy programs; faculty members to conduct instruction through electronic means such as a live telephone or video network; and speakers for a conference or workshop.

These and other "teachers" are recruited daily for adult programs. As prospective instructors, some may have outstanding teaching ability;

others will have a high degree of professional experience or content knowledge but relatively little proficiency with teaching procedures. Among the effective teachers, some will use mainly a didactic approach, others will engage learners in a highly participatory experience, and some will have a broad range of expertise that incorporates the whole continuum of teaching methodology. Some will have no experience in working with adults, while others will have extensive experience. A broadly based continuing education program will find all these people useful. Above all, the staff recruiter will be looking for proficiency in a field of knowledge, teaching ability, and the ability to relate to the individual adult learner.

Specifications for Recruiting Teachers

Before the process of recruiting teachers for a program can begin, the administrator needs to decide what kinds of persons he or she is seeking. The philosophy and expectations of the administrator, the philosophy of the organization or institution, the nature of the content, the nature of the audience, and the kind of instructional processes to be used are all key factors in determining the kind of person to be sought and ultimately the kind of program to be offered. Whomever the administrator selects as teachers will, in effect, become the program.

Administrator's Philosophy. The administrator has a philosophy of continuing education that influences the recruitment and selection process. It may not be written down, it may not be expressed very well, but it is there, and his or her work in continuing education is guided by it. For example, each administrator has a personal conception of the nature of effective teachers and adult learners.

Many of us, however, would have difficulty if someone asked us to write down our philosophy of continuing education. Nevertheless, written statements of philosophy and the mission of the organization provide guidance and an established framework for program development. In addition, it will be helpful to potential teachers to understand the mission and philosophy of the program, because it will help them determine whether or not they wish to join the program.

Job Expectations. It would also be helpful to write down what we expect teachers to do in the classroom, how they should relate to students, what their administrative tasks are, what they do that affects the overall program—in short, a written job description. In the entire recruitment process, it is important that there be a well-defined set of qualifications and expectations for the prospective teacher. The full-time teaching position is clearly one for which a job description ought to be written. Job descriptions for both full-time and part-time teachers can be useful in the recruitment process as a means for communicating the exact specifications of the kind of person desired. A written job description is also important for the applicant as well as for those who serve as references for applicants in getting an accurate picture of what is expected. Later, the written job description can be useful in making decisions on selection and retention.

In situations where instructors are recruited for short-term teaching assignments (such as a conference presentation), a written job description is impractical. However, the administrator must clearly define and communicate what is expected of the instructor in that teaching assignment.

Characteristics of Teachers. Administrators have identified the following qualities as important in selecting teachers: a thorough knowledge of the subject, an attractive personality, skill in using a variety of instructional techniques, flexibility and adaptability in teaching, thorough preparation as teachers, empathy with the adult student, practical experience, cooperativeness, and ability to learn new skills (Kempfer, 1955). The list can be extensive, depending on the situation for which the teacher is being recruited. The actual process of selection is described in the next chapter, but these characteristics are also important considerations in the recruitment process.

Characteristics of Students. The administrator's view of the nature of adult students assists in planning programs and in deciding on the kind of teacher needed. The distinctive characteristics of adult students have been described by several writers.

Whipple (1957), for example, identified six characteristics: the adult has a broader range of experience, emotional meanings for adults are usually outside the experience of youth, adult patterns of thought tend to be fixed, the time perspective of adults is different, the time available for engaging in educational experiences varies, and the motivations of adults are complex and tend to be practical.

More recently, in postulating the theory of andragogy, Knowles (1970) cited four assumptions about adult learners that are different from the assumptions about children as learners. As people mature, their self-concept moves from dependency toward self-direction, they accumulate a growing reservoir of experience, they become oriented to the developmental tasks of their social roles, their time perspective changes from one of postponed application of knowledge to immediacy of application, and accordingly their orientation toward learning shifts from one of subject-centeredness to one of problem-centeredness.

While a given view of the adult learner may stress certain characteristics in favor of others, there is general agreement that those cited above are at least the dominant ones affecting the ways in which teachers relate to adults in educational activities. The recruiter of teachers for adults commonly looks for teachers who understand that adults are different from children and who can apply those understandings in the teaching situation.

Content Versus Process. When a teacher prepares a course for adults, there are at least two basic approaches that may be taken; one emphasizes content, the other emphasizes process or method. In both instances, of course, one is not considered to the exclusion of the other, but they do represent extremes and provide a perspective from which to consider overemphasis on one or the other (Whipple, 1957).

The history of adult education is replete with examples of this controversy, and it is not settled yet. An analysis helpful in finding one's way through the controversy was developed by Coolie Verner (1962), and a broader discussion, entitled "Managing the Learning Experience," appears in Verner and Booth (1964, pp. 68-90).

Verner's conceptual framework defines, describes, and organizes the methods, techniques, and devices used in adult education. In his terms, "a method establishes a relationship between the learner and the institution or agency through which the educational task is accomplished" (Verner and Booth, 1964, p. 68). Major subcategories are individual methods, group methods, and community methods. Techniques, however, are the ways in which the teacher "establishes a relationship between the learner and the learning task" (Verner and Booth, 1964, p. 75). The classification system is based on the appropriateness of a given technique for accomplishing a particular task. Tasks include the acquisition of information, the acquisition of skills, and the application of knowledge. Devices are a variety of instructional aids that increase the effectiveness of methods and techniques. There are illustrative devices (such as demonstrations and films), extension devices (such as radio and television), environmental devices (such as movable seating), and manipulative devices (such as tools and equipment).

In seeking effective teachers, a determining factor may well be the kind of situation in which the person will teach. If a person is being recruited into a program that is already established and uses a specific methodology, such as face-to-face group instruction, correspondence instruction, intensive human relations seminars, instruction by television, or tutorial instruction, it will be important to select individuals who have not only the required content expertise but also the ability to work effectively with the specific methodology. However, the recruiter who works in a program that uses a variety of processes will select teachers who collectively utilize a variety of methods, techniques, and devices in their teaching. Each educational process and each content area impose their own limitations and opportunities.

Sources of Teachers

Experienced recruiters never stop recruiting—they are ever alert to the unforeseen opportunity to recruit a new teacher. But there are also numerous basic sources to which recruiters can turn as they search systematically for instructors. What we really want to acquire is a pool of effective teachers from which we can select those we need, and to do this effectively the net may need to be cast very widely. The number of places to look for teachers is limited only by the creative mind of the continuing educator.

The source for finding a particular teacher will depend on the nature of the teaching assignment. If the teacher is being sought for a long-term program—one that will take place over several weeks or months, such as a public school evening course, a correspondence course, or a community discussion group—it will probably be best to seek a local person who lives within a few miles of the instructional site. However, if an instructor or resource person is being recruited for a short-term program a few days in length, such as a conference, workshop, tour, or perhaps a short college summer session, the selection can be made from regional, national, and even international sources.

The following list of sources suggests some of the types of people, institutions, organizations, experiences, and documents from which potential teachers can be identified. While not exhaustive, it is an initial source that continuing educators can use for brainstorming in developing a list particularly relevant to their programs. Selection of any of these sources will depend in great measure on the purpose for which an instructor is sought. Therefore in the list below specific examples have been suggested in order to relate to the everyday practice of continuing educators.

Printed Documents. There are many documents that, though often overlooked, can provide the practitioner with information about possible sources of teachers. In some instances documents provide the names and addresses of people or organizations who can refer administrators to teachers. In other cases, prospective teachers can be identified directly from the information provided.

Newspapers offer at least three types of opportunities for recruiting. First, they are prime sources of what is happening in a community, a region, the nation, or the world. Feature stories in particular may identify citizens who have special capabilities or interests that may qualify them for teaching. In addition to local papers, many libraries maintain subscriptions to the *New York Times,* the *Wall Street Journal,* and various specialized papers. The *New York Times Index* can be a prime source of information about people and current topics. Second, a news story about the program may alert prospective teachers to teaching opportunities. Third, the administrator can place an advertisement in the classified section of papers to recruit local teachers.

Publications of organizations, such as professional, trade, or voluntary associations, not only indicate topics of current interest to the membership but also persons who have recognized expertise in specific areas. Newsletters often indicate who is doing new things or has special interests. Nearly all academic fields of specialization publish journals or books written by experts, who thus become prime candidates for involvement as resource persons or speakers in seminars, conferences, or other activities.

Brochures and catalogs of other continuing education programs may suggest not only new courses for your own program but also speakers or instructors. One needs to be sensitive, however, in using instructors of other local programs, especially if the person is to teach the same course at your institution. Occasionally cooperative arrangements can be made in which the person teaches for both programs but teaches different topics.

Reference books abound in many fields, and most city or institutional libraries will have at least some. The Gale Research Company publishes several current reference works that list organizations, people, and information sources in a variety of fields. One example is their *Encyclopedia of Associations* (Fisk, 1977), which lists thousands of professional, trade, educational, and other associations, regional, national and international in scope, with a geographical and executive officer index. A phone call or letter to an association's headquarters can often provide information on printed as well as on human resources. In our own field the *Handbook of Adult Education* (Smith, Aker, and Kidd, 1970) has information on program areas, a directory of organizations in adult education, and a list of general information sources. Many other fields or organizations have similar publications. The American Society for Training and Development publishes two documents of interest to recruiters. The *Training and Development Handbook* (Craig, 1976) contains a wealth of information about human resource development written by specialists, and *Who's Who in Training and Development, 1979* lists the society's national membership, a rich resource of trainers as well as referrals to specialists in a variety of fields. A reference book often overlooked is the local telephone directory; the Yellow Pages include a cross-indexed subject listing of primarily commercial enterprises that may specialize in a service or product related to a continuing education program. For example, the proprietor of a local hobby store might be a teacher for a model airplane engine clinic.

With the increased use of computers, a natural outgrowth has been the development of a large number of data banks that are easily accessible to the general public. Many libraries, particularly those associated with universities and colleges, now have direct computer access capability to search an extensive array of bibliographic data bases. Many industrial firms, especially those with research components, also have "on-line" access to the same data bases. In general use throughout the United States are two systems—the DIALOG service of Lockheed Missile and Space Co. and the ORBIT service of System Development Corporation. Collectively, these have over 125 data bases covering published material and data in virtually all subject areas. Searches, when carefully done, can be quite inexpensive—often costing as little as ten or fifteen dollars. While these systems may have limited usefulness to most recruiters, it is easy to imagine that a person interested in convening a major international symposium on recent research in adult learning, for example, might search the Educational Resources Information Center (ERIC) system to find out who is doing research in that area as a first step in developing a preliminary invitation list. Someone interested in a conference on the physical sciences could search the Smithsonian Scientific Information Exchange (SSIE) data base on current research. An informative article on how to search the ERIC system, which is similar to most other systems, has been written by Grabowski (1976).

Surveys of groups that may contain prospective teachers are a somewhat formal method of locating potential teachers for adult programs. Gowin and Daigneault (1961) have reported on two surveys that were used to locate and subsequently recruit teachers for a broadly based evening college program. The first was a survey of selected organizations in a local community whose members were deemed likely to have college degrees and an interest in teaching. The groups included the local chapter of the American Association of University Women, the local medical association, a regional personnel association, the alumni chapters of two nearby private colleges, the local chapter of the Society for the Advancement of Management, and the local chapter of Phi Beta Kappa. A list of potential part-time teachers was compiled, and 1,445 letters were sent to citizens. In addition, managers of research groups in local industries were contacted.

The letter to citizens briefly described the program and asked individuals to respond with a postcard indicating interest, whether they would be willing to complete a personal data form, and whether, if selected, they would be willing to participate in a preservice training program. Of the 277 people who completed personal data forms, 139 (50 percent) held master's, LL.B.'s, or doctoral degrees. Respondents whose backgrounds were in arts and sciences, business administration, and engineering indicated the greatest interest. Many people had several years of professional experience as well as teaching experience. Approximately 60 percent were deemed appropriate by the deans of the colleges to be interviewed if vacancies should occur.

A second survey was developed and distributed to 200 employees of a major industrial research laboratory, a type of organization that typically employs scientists and researchers with extensive academic qualifications, similar to those desired by colleges and universities for full-time faculty. Of the 200 surveyed, 128 employees responded affirmatively to a question about their interest in part-time teaching on released time. Furthermore, 65 percent of those who responded indicated an interest in receiving preservice training. Necessarily, a released time arrangement with local industry requires the cooperation of industrial firms, and a subsequent survey of a sample of American industrial research laboratories indicated that there was substantial interest in cooperative arrangements, although there were some disadvantages cited, such as a possible conflict of interest or interference with the normal work assignments of laboratory employees.

Human Sources. The types of people who can provide information about potential teachers are almost endless. The following list contains some people so obvious that they may be overlooked and others who would be helpful only in specialized situations. They lend themselves to no classification system.

Within one's own organization is the first place to look, both for prospective teachers and for people who can suggest others who may be teachers or who can suggest potential teachers. A review of the files of resumes of current and former staff members may indicate hobbies, special interests, or previous employment experience that may qualify them for new course or program offerings. Current teaching, program, and administrative staff may also be able to make referrals to people who have special capabilities.

Investigate the possibilities of securing part-time teachers from other local, regional, or national organizations similar in mission to yours. If resources are being recruited for short-term programs, organizations in other parts of the country may have specialists available for brief periods of time.

Most educational institutions, such as public schools, community colleges, and universities, usually look first to their own regular or daytime faculty or administrators for part-time instructors for both credit and noncredit programs for adults. Many, however, will utilize people in the community at large who have appropriate educational credentials for a portion of their instructional staff. Noncredit programs tend to use a higher proportion of community resources than do academic credit programs. Referrals are often made by department heads and other administrators as well as by teaching colleagues. College and university alumni, particularly those who have graduated from professional schools and have become specialists, are another source of teachers. Graduate students are also potential teachers for continuing education programs.

Community resources, which may be approached directly or through organized groups, include business and industrial firms, members of various professions (doctors, lawyers, public accountants, dentists), and officers of community and voluntary organizations (churches, United Way, neighborhood groups, recreation or leisure groups). Many national or regional associations have local affiliates that can provide teachers, referrals, and information about and even contacts with national figures. Government offices at all levels—local, state, regional, and national—often have specialists in the subject matter of the agency and are eager to have their staff members participate in educational programs. Some examples of local government offices with resources include community development, public safety, recreation, office of the mayor or city manager, commission on the status of women, and the Comprehensive Employment Training Act (CETA) office.

Some administrators make it a practice to attend as many gatherings as possible, and in the process they discover potential teachers at luncheons, meetings, conferences, or conventions. The advantage here is that one may have an opportunity to observe persons in leadership roles and can make at least a preliminary judgment about their abilities in teaching a group of people and their grasp of subject matter.

Another approach is to contact known experts who may not themselves be available but can refer you to someone else who is. This is a fairly common practice among people planning conferences.

Groups of people often overlooked as referral sources are magazine editors and newspaper, television, and radio reporters. They frequently come in contact with people who have special interests and abilities and may be willing to provide the names of such people.

Advisory committees can be an important part of teacher recruitment. University conference departments, for instance, frequently establish temporary program planning committees whose responsibilities include the identification of instructional resources as well as overall program development. On a more permanent basis, many organizations have established program advisory committees to provide continuous advice and support with attention to special program needs such as recruiting teachers and other resource people.

Another source of teachers is the readership of your program catalog or schedule. Invitations to prospective teachers to submit proposals for courses or workshops are sometimes published in schedules or other documents.

Perhaps the final source of teachers that might be mentioned is the teacher who approaches the program administrator with fresh ideas for courses he or she would like to teach. In many instances these are extremely well-qualified people, perhaps new to the community, who have heard about the program and would like to teach in it. Often they have taught similar courses at other institutions. Sometimes their idea is an offshoot of their regular work or teaching efforts. Faculty members, for example, may want to experiment with some instructional ideas in a noncredit course before introducing them formally into the institution's curriculum. As the program grows in visibility and credibility, more and more offers of assistance will be received. Most offers are legitimate and well-intentioned, but occasionally you will be the beneficiary of people who see the program as a vehicle for promulgating their own peculiar view of mankind or mankind's place in the world, or for implementing their ideas because they have been blocked elsewhere. Needless to say, such offers should be evaluated very carefully, and this may include some reference checks one would not ordinarily make.

A Recruitment Plan

While recruitment is clearly a continuous process in which the effective administrator is always alert to potential programs and prospective teachers, there may also be a need in selected programs to approach recruiting in a systematic fashion, in much the same way that program development is a systematic process. The university evening college or the YMCA winter term program in which most events will begin at about the same time, for example, may find that a recruiting plan carried out in a specific time period is most effective. In other situations, such as those encountered by independent study programs where students can enroll at any time, or in conference operations where programs begin every day of the week throughout the year, it is not possible to concentrate the staff recruiting process into a specific time period. Thus, a recruitment plan should be flexible in order to respond to the varied needs of individual activities within a larger program and to the changing needs of a diverse program.

Whether the recruitment process is concentrated into a limited number of time periods each year or is a continuous effort, there are certain common elements that can make the process more effective: specification of the kinds of teachers needed; the sources of teachers; recruiting methods; a time schedule; mechanisms for distributing recruitment notices; procedures for processing applications, selecting applicants, and appointing teachers; and evaluation of the recruitment plan. Individual steps in the recruitment process may be more helpful in some kinds of searches than in others, and therefore administrators will need to adapt the plan to their specific situation. Several of these elements have been discussed earlier, and others will be presented in later chapters; thus, the following discussion attempts to show the interrelationships among the parts of the whole plan and describes in detail only those elements not discussed elsewhere.

Specifications. The search for teachers depends on the kinds of teachers needed, the personal and professional characteristics of teachers deemed appropriate and desirable by the individual institution and administrator, and the nature of the student body. In developing specifications for recruiting, a job description for each position is desirable. The job description should include the nature of the teaching assignment (such as part-time or evenings), the minimum educational qualifications, the professional or practical experience necessary, the specific tasks performed, relationships within the organization, the subject matter to be taught, the teaching skills needed or instructional methods to be used if specific requirements exist, and any professional or teaching certificates required.

Sources. From among the range of possible sources of teachers, those that seem most appropriate for each position available should be selected.

Recruitment Methods. For the best results, it is probably desirable to approach specific sources in a particular manner. For instance, in the initial stages of a search and depending on the number of teachers needed, it may be desirable to communicate personally with some key sources to alert them to your needs, followed by a letter or other written document that provides detailed job specifications. In developing this step of the recruitment plan, identify each of the methods to be used for securing applicants for each position. In identifying sources of applicants and recruitment methods, it is helpful to identify some "fall back" options in case the first options are not productive.

Time Schedule. Early in the development of the recruitment plan, construct a reverse calendar time schedule that shows both the steps in the recruitment plan and the date by which each step must be accomplished. For example, assume that you are planning the fall schedule and that about one hundred activities will be offered, of which eighty are continuing from previous terms. For the eighty continuing courses, sixty-five will be taught by the current faculty but fifteen new teachers need to be recruited. Thus you need to recruit a total of about thirty-five new faculty. The reverse time calendar might appear as follows:

Date	Task
September 1	Classes start
August 1	Program schedule mailed
July 1	Program schedule to printer
June 1	All activities scheduled and teaching assignments made
April 1–May 31	Select and appoint teachers
February 15–May 1	Carry out recruiting effort
January 1–February 28	Identify programs to be offered and consequent teaching needs; develop job descriptions and prepare recruiting materials

This time schedule would vary, of course, depending on the scope and complexity of the task. It would also vary depending on the traditions of the agency. For instance, if appointments of part-time evening college faculty require approval by full-time regular faculty, the process might be somewhat longer and involve more steps.

Note that recruiting starts while the present term's activities are underway and is not completed until after the present term has ended. With this schedule, plans for the next term can be adjusted for classes that were canceled due to low enrollment or to replace teachers who will not be reemployed because of poor performance. Institutions that are on a quarter system may find that they do not have the luxury of knowing what classes have been canceled or what teachers will not perform adequately before they must complete the plans for the next term. In this situation the administrator will always be a term behind in dealing with such decisions as they affect the course offerings.

In carrying out the recruitment process, it is always useful to identify more teachers than are needed, because inevitably someone will move out of town, become ill, or for any number of reasons not be available at the last minute for a teaching assignment. You always need well-qualified substitutes, and the substitute list may fill next term's vacancy.

Distribution of Recruiting Notices. Vacancy notices should be based on the job description with as much specificity as possible and should also indicate the location of the assignment, where to apply, the required and desired abilities and experience, and any applicable federal, state, or institutional regulations, such as affirmative action or equal opportunity. Notices may be mailed or delivered to the sources determined earlier, and advertisements placed in newspapers, journals, newsletters, or other appropriate publications. This should be accomplished far enough in advance so that applicants have substantial time to respond.

Processing Applications. Applications should be acknowledged promptly. A process should be established for reviewing each application in such a manner that a pool of the best qualified applicants, based on the criteria established, is created for each position.

Selection and Appointment of Teachers. Selection is perhaps the most crucial step in the entire staffing process. This function is described in detail by Conti and Porter in a later chapter.

Evaluation of Recruitment Plan. After recruitment has been completed and the schedule has been sent to the printer, the process should be reviewed and its strengths and weaknesses identified. The basic question is how well did it work. Did it generate enough people from which the kinds of teachers needed for the program could be selected? What sources proved to be best? Was the time allowed in the schedule adequate? Were the specifications and notices adequate, or did they attract a large number of people who were clearly unqualified? How can the process be made more efficient and more productive?

Summary

Recruiting teachers for continuing education programs is a continuous and important aspect of adult education programming. The basic recruitment task is to create a pool of well-qualified applicants from which effective teachers can be selected. There is a multitude of sources, both human and documentary, available to the inquisitive recruiter, whether he or she is seeking a local, national, or international resource person. It is important to develop a programming philosophy as a prelude to specifying and recruiting the kind of teachers needed. The recruitment plan should be developed accordingly, allowing sufficient time to carry out the entire selection process before deadlines arrive. The innovative recruiter will always be searching, because good teachers are where you find them, and whomever you select as teachers will in effect become your program.

References

Craig, R. L. (Ed.). *Training and Development Handbook.* (2nd ed.) New York: McGraw-Hill, 1976.
Fisk, M. (Ed.). *Encyclopedia of Associations.* (11th ed.) Detroit: Gale Research Co., 1977.
Gowin, D. B., and Daigneault, G. H. *The Part-Time College Teacher.* Chicago: Center for the Study of Liberal Education for Adults, 1961.
Grabowski, S. M. "How a Trainer Can Use ERIC." *Training and Development Journal,* 1976, *30* (4), 28-31.
Kempfer, H. *Adult Education.* New York: McGraw-Hill, 1955.
Knowles, M. S. *The Modern Practice of Adult Education.* New York: Association Press, 1970.
Sheldon, J. A., and Wasinger, G. B. "Selection of Teachers, Leaders, and Other Supportive Staff." In N. C. Shaw (Ed.), *Administration of Continuing Education.* Washington, D.C.: National Association for Public School Adult Education, 1969.
Smith, R. M., Aker, G. F., and Kidd, J. R. (Eds.). *Handbook of Adult Education.* New York: Macmillan, 1970.
Stanton, S. "The Sequential Selection System: The Key to Hiring Better People." *Training and Development Journal,* 1979, *33* (3), 60-62.
Verner, C. *A Conceptual Scheme for the Identification and Classification of Processes for Adult Education.* Chicago: Adult Education Association of the U.S.A., 1962.
Verner, C., and Booth, A. *Adult Education.* Washington, D.C.: Center for Applied Research in Education, 1964.
Whipple, J. B. *Especially for Adults.* Notes and Essays on Education for Adults, No. 19. Chicago: Center for the Study of Liberal Education for Adults, 1957.
Who's Who in Training and Development, 1979. Madison, Wisc.: American Society for Training and Development, 1979.

John H. Buskey is associate dean of continuing studies and assistant professor of adult and continuing education at the University of Nebraska-Lincoln. He was formerly the director of conferences and institutes at the University of Maryland University College.

*Making wise decisions in selecting teachers requires a
detailed and sophisticated approach.*

The Selection Process

Gary J. Conti
Lee Porter

Qualified teachers for continuing education programs must be identified and hired. Most continuing education administrators would sleep more soundly if all their teachers possessed proficiency in their subject matter area, displayed a keen interest in their students, submitted reports on time, demonstrated their knowledge of the needs of adult learners, and provided evidence of their skill in educational methods. While these features are not meant to be criteria, they show that qualifications for teachers cover many aspects of proficiency, including knowledge, skills, and attitudes. The challenge is to select teachers who rank high in these areas.

Selection involves screening potential teachers and identifying those who are willing and able to do the job well. The staffing responsibility for part-time teaching staff usually rests with the program administrator. Often the administrator must make a decision within a short space of time, with minimal help from departmental screening committees, and without the time or resources for miniteaching sessions or the technical aid of videotaped microteaching. To make an informed decision intelligently and to maximize the chances of placing an effective teacher in each class, the administrator must have a thorough understanding of the educational environment and the selection process, have pertinent data-gathering devices, and be effective in analyzing data and making decisions.

The Educational Environment

The concept of educational environment includes the institutional mission, the administrator's philosophy, the nature of the course content, the nature of the potential audience, and the unique external variables affecting the institution, such as government guidelines. Before evaluating potential teachers, the selecting administrator must be aware of these factors and their interrelationships.

Institutional Mission. Continuing education often functions as a division within a parent organization. As a result, its operational procedures and personnel selections can be influenced by the particular curriculum tradition and philosophy of the organization. Blaney (1974) has identified three basic patterns of curricular authority that can influence the selection of staff. In one pattern, organizations view their role as carefully prescribing what the adult student is to learn. In the second pattern, the organization invites the learners to participate in the decisions about the program and its implementation. In the third pattern, organizations place the responsibility for program development directly with the student. In practice, all three patterns may exist to some degree in a large organization such as a state university.

Although the same elements of setting objectives, exercising authority, selecting procedures, and evaluating and conducting learning activities are carried out in each pattern, they receive differing emphases and expression in each (Smith, 1976). It is therefore the responsibility of the continuing education administrator to identify the program development approach of his or her organization and to assess the implications of this approach for the implementation of the continuing education program.

Administrator's Philosophy. There are essentially two philosophical approaches, each of which calls for a different type of teacher and a different approach to staffing. In one approach the teacher's role is dominant in directing the learner. The educator designs and offers a preconstructed package to the incoming learners. Learners must accept and adjust to the learning experiences designed by the "trustees of knowledge." The second approach emphasizes problem-solving experiences that are relevant to the learner. The role of the teacher is to serve as a facilitator who exposes learners to experiences that can be applied to future problem-solving activities. Some administrators may be operating from either one position or the other, and their selection of teachers may be influenced accordingly. Other administrators may operate in an eclectic manner and base their decisions on the nature of the course or the individuals who are expected to enroll.

Nature of the Course Content. Courses designed to introduce new concepts or procedures or clarify material may efficiently utilize lecturers. Courses emphasizing student initiative, reflective thinking, and creative expression demand teachers effective in group dynamics and discussion leadership. It is therefore necessary to analyze the content and educational objectives for each course and select the most effective method of instruction for delivering them. The staffing problem then becomes one of selecting the most qualified person who not only has strong academic preparation in the content area but is also proficient in the most appropriate instructional mode.

Nature of the Potential Audience. Adult educators have long been aware that students participate in continuing education activities for a variety of reasons. Houle (1961) introduced the concept of learning orientations, which generally holds that adults participate in learning activities in order to gain knowledge that will assist them in accomplishing a goal, for social reasons unrelated to the purposes or content of the educational activity, or to quench their desire to know. Burgess (1971) and others have further delineated these categories. Boshier (1971; 1974) found motivation more complex than the orientations outlined in these studies and identified additional motivational factors. He concluded that adult participants in continuing education are motivated by either growth or deficiency and that "the onus for matching participants and educational environments rests with administrators organizing educational experience for adults" (Boshier, 1974, p. 279).

Cross (1976) has pointed out that learners have characteristic styles for collecting and gathering information. These distinct methods of using the mind are termed *cognitive styles*. While psychologists have discussed several cognitive dimensions, the cognitive styles of field-dependent and field-independent have received the most attention. Research in these areas indicates that students make sense of course material in different ways and that "in general, people will probably be happier and more productive if they are studying or teaching via a method compatible with their style" (Cross, 1976, p. 130). Research further suggests that learners with similar cognitive styles may be attracted to certain programs, while learners with certain styles may purposely avoid specific programs. The administrators must therefore ensure that staffing is not systematically biased in favor of a particular cognitive style and that staff members provide alternative approaches to learning for students whose cognitive styles are not especially well suited to the specific academic content of the course (Solomon, Bezdek, and Rosenberg, 1963).

Unique External Variables. These include the availability of well-trained personnel, the population of the area, the reputation of the institution, the pay scale, and the length of time before the class starts.

Government Guidelines. The intention of the guidelines on affirmative action and equal opportunity is not questioned on the basis of the long-term benefits and opportunities they provide for women and minorities. While these procedures do influence and improve the selection process, considerable time can be consumed in meeting the specified requirements. Some organizations, especially those which receive a large number of grants from the government or those with large government contracts, must conform very closely to the guidelines. Adhering to these regulations often involves recording data on the exact number of women and minorities who apply and interview for the position. Also, as discussed later in this chapter, there are suggested guidelines on the composition of search committees. So, regardless of the size of the organization, the alert administrator should adjust the procedures as needed so that they are consistent with affirmative action policies before the selection process begins.

Consequently there are many variables that affect the selection process, and they combine differently in each situation. However, astute administrators are aware of the variables, consciously analyze them, and assign each the proper weight in the formula for identifying the most appropriate teacher.

Aids in the Selection Process

After synthesizing the data concerning organizational characteristics, the administrator is ready to gather information for the assessment of applicants. If there are only three or four applicants for a position, it may be appropriate to proceed immediately to the interview stage of the selection process. However, it has been common in recent years to receive dozens, if not hundreds, of applications for a desirable teaching position. Interviewing more than seven people can be extremely time-consuming and costly. Thus the following preinterview steps can be used.

Search Committees. These committees can serve many useful purposes. Besides saving the administrator a considerable amount of time, they add a dimension of objectivity to the screening process. For example, a committee consisting of individuals with varying backgrounds and interests will introduce unique sets of interests, values, and knowledge. This blend of input should assure the administrator that the ultimate selection was made with optimum fairness and objectivity. Search committees may be a requirement in some organizations.

A productive search committee can assist the administrator in almost every stage of the selection activity. In addition to reviewing resumes, references, and other data submitted by the applicants, committee members can contact references and take part in the interviews.

The composition of the committee is an important administrative decision. Unless the members are accessible and committed, the value of the committee is limited. Also, regardless of affirmative action policies, it is wise to strengthen a committee by having a wide range of backgrounds in terms of age, sex, race, education, and work experience. It is recognized, of course, that representation from all minority groups, old and young, male and female, and various educational levels would result in a committee of fifteen to twenty people. This is not workable; effective committees usually have three to seven members.

Checking References. Assuming a functioning search committee has screened the applicants by comparing backgrounds with the stated criteria for the position and assuming one or more of the candidates has met these criteria (on paper), other steps can be taken to collect additional information. Checking references can yield valuable information. Although some administrators prefer to take this step after the interview, it is possible to save time by making calls before the candidate meets with the administrator. Unless indicated otherwise, it is customary to assume that the candidate approves of direct contact with the references supplied on the resume or application form. In any case, calling references can often produce information that has been excluded in letters of recommendation. Besides the fact that most such letters include only positive attributes, the phone call permits the administrator to ask specific questions about the candidate's strengths and weaknesses.

Observation Techniques. In spite of the usual time pressures faced by the administrator, other techniques should be used if possible. For instance, if the candidate is currently teaching in another setting, it could be enlightening to visit the classroom. Or, as is often the case in recent years, the candidate may have videotapes of classroom performance. It is also appropriate to ask the candidate to prepare a special lecture or seminar as a method of evaluating his or her teaching proficiency. All three of the above mentioned observation techniques permit the administrator to witness and evaluate performance.

Written Instruments. These may be useful in the data collection stage and can facilitate the decision-making process by providing valuable information. Unfortunately, a recent search of the continuing education literature indicates a paucity of instruments specifically designed for this purpose. Two instruments that do have potential for yielding useful data in the screening process are the Principles of Adult Learning Scale (Conti, 1978) and the Educational Orientation Questionnaire (Hadley, 1975). Although both were developed for use in empirical research, they may be used to elicit data concerning the teacher's preferred instructional mode and philosophical orientation. These data can in turn be matched against the variables in the educational environment that have already been identified by the administrator. This information may thus help identify the most compatible prospects for each course and may provide significant discussion items to help focus the interview.

The Principles of Adult Learning Scale (PALS) is a forty-four-item instrument that measures the degree of teacher preference for the collaborative teaching-learning mode. Historically, the collaborative mode, which is defined as the learner-centered method of instruction in which authority for curriculum formation is shared by the learner and the practitioner, has received wide support in the continuing education literature. PALS asks prospective teachers to indicate the frequency with which they practice various classroom behaviors. Each respondent's score can be ranked on a continuum and viewed as an indicator of his or her preference for actions that either stimulate learner initiative or restrict student responses.

The Educational Orientation Questionnaire is a sixty-item instrument that assesses an educator's orientation to the constructs of andragogy and pedagogy. The examinees are asked to respond in six attitudinal dimensions to statements about education, teaching, and learning, producing scores that indicate the degree of a teacher's andragogical orientation.

Although both instruments are designed for research purposes, they are capable of providing useful data quickly for the administrator in charge of the screening process. Both are also easy to score. Both provide information about important constructs that must be considered in the screening process and a relative ranking of an individual's preferences, feelings, and commitments concerning these concepts. Instruments such as these can aid the administrator in identifying a pool of potential teachers who satisfy the predefined characteristics for a particular course. Equipped with this information and other data, the administrator is ready for the interviewing process.

The Interview

Resumes, reference letters, lists of publications, patents, professional achievements, and cover letters supply valuable information about a potential teacher, but the interview is the decisive stage in screening and selection. The interview can be a meaningless formality or an opportunity to collect information, appraise talents, and probe for further information and insight.

Regrettably, there is no easy formula that outlines the interviewing process. Just as psychological tests have limited validity and reliability, interviews gather only a limited sample of the potential teacher's capability. Therefore the administrator's judgment is fundamental in the selection process.

Getting Started. As has been stated, it is the interviewer's responsibility to have a precise understanding of the educational environment. From this frame of reference he or she can decide on each applicant's suitability for the position by focusing on the applicant's educational preparation, knowledge of content, and teaching style. Attention must be given to the appropriateness of credentials and how current is the candidate's knowledge and skill in the subject taught. For example, consider the danger of hiring a 1960 Ph.D. graduate in computer science to teach a seminar for practicing data-processing hardware specialists. The instructor has fine credentials but only a well-structured interview can show how current he or she is in a rapidly changing field.

The most fruitful interviews result from a clear and detailed specification of the position and of the type of person desired to fill that opening. Unfortunately it is not always easy to set exact specifications. The administrator may wish to seek assistance in defining interviewing objectives. One useful method is to meet with other teachers of adults, especially those in the same or similar disciplines, to decide what elements need to be pursued in an interview and the relative importance of the types of information gathered. Of course there will not be total accord among the other instructors about the necessary qualities, but the different perceptions will provide guidelines and help broaden the interviewer's perspective.

In summary, the best judgments are usually made when the interviewer has appropriate and accurate information about the candidate. Effective planning is essential to bring objectivity and awareness to the appraisal.

The Setting. Privacy, confidentiality, relaxation, and rapport are important in interviews, since interviews are stressful events for most people regardless of their educational background or achievements. Privacy generally enhances and encourages freedom of expression. Maintaining a confidential relationship during the interview helps the candidate feel more secure and can encourage conversation that better represents his or her behavior. Relaxation can also reduce stress. The candidate is more likely to supply the necessary responses when there is no fear that the interview will end abruptly. Above all, the skilled interviewer should give the impression that there is plenty of time and avoid interruptions such as telephone calls. An initial effort to establish a congenial atmosphere is essential; this can be easily accomplished by means of general conversation about a social topic unrelated to the job, in order to help the applicant feel relaxed. The right setting is necessary to reduce caution and stimulate a candid and revealing conversation.

Conducting the Interview. The key to effective appraisal during the interview is listening. Regrettably, interviewers often forget the value of listening for both the interviewer and the applicant. There is a tendency for administrators to try to sell themselves, their programs, and their institutions. This common failing of interviewers lessens the value of the interview in at least two ways. First, it does not give the applicant an opportunity to experience the therapeutic value of being listened to or to fully explain his or her ideas, experiences, and strengths. Second, the interviewer cannot assess the relative strengths and weaknesses of the candidate. For without listening, the interviewer cannot judge the quality of responses, probe for further information, and separate the important from the unimportant.

The stress on listening should not be interpreted to mean that only the administrator is performing an evaluation exercise. Obviously, the sophisticated applicant is appraising the administrator and the organization. Yet the main purpose of the interview is to decide whether the applicant will enhance the instructional program of the organization. The emphasis on listening does not suggest a passive role for the interviewer. The interviewer must direct the interview and cover in detail the necessary topics in order to make a sound judgment about the applicant's qualifications.

Should the interviewer use direct or indirect questions? Should he or she ask, "Are you a good teacher?" or, "What are your strong points as a teacher?" Although this is a matter of interviewing style and preference, the indirect method usually provides more valuable information. It also gives the applicant a chance to interpret the question and to develop a point of view without being threatened or locked into a yes or no response.

There is a tendency among interviewers to answer questions for the applicants. For example, if the interviewer asks the applicant to comment on his or her perceptions of the needs of the adult learner and the applicant gives a one-sentence response, it is quite common for the interviewer to expand on the applicant's response. However, we recommend that the applicant be encouraged instead to elaborate on his or her response. This can usually be accomplished by interjecting an expression of agreement or requesting a more extensive answer. Sometimes it is necessary to urge the applicant to continue by saying to him or her, "Go on," "And then?" or "Can you tell me more about that?"

Another technique for securing more information is simply to restate what the applicant has said. This gives the interviewee an opportunity to recognize the lack of clarity or detail in the original response. It also provides a stimulus for elaborating on the point in question.

Finally, the personal interview is an extremely expensive technique for collecting information. Therefore the interviewer should take full advantage of the time available. While listening carefully is essential and urging elaboration on certain points is helpful, it must be remembered that verbal communication has certain limitations. Therefore the successful interviewer should note gestures, expressions, manners, and pauses. It is especially important to search for patterns in relation to long pauses. Do they occur in response to certain types of questions? In any case, the interviewer should resist answering for the candidate because the only way to make judgments about the applicant's knowledge, skill, and attitudes is to keep him or her talking.

The Final Judgment. Given that the best judgments are made when there is objectivity and sufficient data, the interviewer should try to avoid the following errors.

Like me. There is a tendency to react positively to applicants who have characteristics similar to those of the interviewer. Whether this is a conscious or unconscious reaction, it distorts one's judgment.

Not like me. There is a similar tendency to react negatively to people who have significantly different characteristics from those of the interviewer. This reaction is equally misleading.

Blind spot. There is a temptation to latch on to one positive attribute and ignore other deficiencies. For example, an interviewer can be so impressed by an applicant's formal education that minimal experience (when experience is called for) is completely overlooked.

Stereotyping. Successful administrators fall into the stereotyping mold as much as other people. It is easy to conclude inaccurately that all accountants have cold personalities or that all Ph.D.'s are too theoretical. One cannot afford to depend on stereotypes when appraising individuals for specific instructional assignments.

Halo effect. Although readily acknowledged as a danger in interviewing, administrators fall victim to this common problem. One excellent quality does not mean that all features are excellent.

There is still more to consider. Did the candidate mention personal problems or uncertainties as well as successes? Was the person honest and realistic in responding to questions? Was he or she unduly nervous? Did it appear that something was being hidden? Was there evidence that the applicant was overly critical? Was he or she too eager?

One cannot conduct an interview as a chemist performs an established experiment; there is no formula. A successful interviewer is more like an inventor. There must be a purpose, a plan, and a critical awareness of what is happening.

Assuming the interviews are completed, the selection process has at least one final step—the decision. All events and factors should be reviewed. Did the members of the search committee reach a consensus? If not, the administrator will have to weigh the differences among the members and compare them with the position criteria. Did the reference checks conform to the judgments made at the interviews? If used, did scores from the written instruments meet the criteria?

Finally, who makes the decision? Is the administrator's selection simply advisory to the director, dean, vice-president, principal or board of directors? Is the search committee's decision final or is it advisory to the administrator? These questions should be answered before the selection process begins.

Summary

Few administrative decisions are as important as the wise selection of qualified teachers. Although administrators may be tempted to "grab" the first promising applicant who appears, the integrity of his or her program dictates a more detailed and sophisticated approach. The essential ingredients in the process are an analysis of the educational environment, a clear statement of the teaching position to be filled, a concise notion of the type of person being sought, knowledge of the institutional and governmental guidelines influencing the selection, techniques for narrowing down the number of candidates, and the basic principles of interviewing and making the final decision.

References

Blaney, J. "Program Development and Curricular Authority." In J. Blaney, I. Housego, and G. McIntosh (Eds.), *A Monograph on Program Development in Education.* Vancouver: University of British Columbia, 1974.

Boshier, R. W. "Motivational Orientations of Adult Education Participants: A Factor Analytic Exploration of Houle's Typology." *Adult Education,* 1971, *21* (2), 3-26.

Boshier, R. W. "Educational Participation and Dropout: A Theoretical Model." *Adult Education,* 1974, *23* (4), 255-282.

Burgess, P. "Reasons for Adult Participation in Group Educational Activities." *Adult Education,* 1971, *22* (1), 3-29.

Conti, G. J. "Principles of Adult Learning Scale: An Instrument for Measuring Teacher Behavior Related to the Collaborative Teaching-Learning Mode." Unpublished doctoral dissertation, Northern Illinois University, 1978.

Cross, K. P. *Accent on Learning.* San Francisco: Jossey-Bass, 1976.

Hadley, H. N. "Development of an Instrument to Determine Adult Educators' Orientation, Andragogical or Pedagogical." Unpublished doctoral dissertation, Boston University, 1975.

Houle, C. O. *The Inquiring Mind.* Madison: University of Wisconsin Press, 1961.

Smith, R. M. *Learning How to Learn in Adult Education.* DeKalb, Ill.: ERIC Clearinghouse in Career Education, 1976.

Solomon, D., Bezdek, W. E., and Rosenberg, L. *Teaching Styles and Learning.* Chicago: Center for the Study of Liberal Education for Adults, 1963.

Dr. Gary J. Conti is the director of evening and continuing education at Spoon River College, Canton, Illinois.

Dr. Lee Porter is dean of the college of continuing education, Roosevelt University in Chicago, Illinois.

*Staff development is no longer a frill that
organizations provide in affluent times. It is a basic
means by which organizations achieve their goals.*

Staff Development: A Mandate for Organizational Survival

Carroll A. Londoner

Staff development is an essential task of continuing education agencies. It is especially important now, since budgetary constraints curtail the hiring of new full-time instructional staff at most educational institutions, while continuing education units find it necessary to increase the number of people who teach part-time. This requires staff development for both full- and part-time teachers.

Rationale for Staff Development

The commitment to staff development is necessary for several reasons. First, staff development is one of the basic means by which an organization achieves its goals. It is in staff development that an organization's goals are interpreted and integrated with the teacher's career goals, as both strive to meet the needs of adult learners. Second, teachers need to be made aware of new knowledge and skills that can enhance their effectiveness with adult learners. The discipline of adult and continuing education is still in the seminal stage of testing and refining various teaching strategies. Staff development thus becomes a major source for disseminating the results of these efforts. Finally, staff development increases the teacher's proficiency in both subject matter and educational processes.

Staff development covers all activities that improve job knowledge, performance, skills, values, and attitudes of employees. It embraces the areas of orientation, in-service education, career-path development, and organizational development and renewal. Thus in its broadest form staff development attempts to match employees' personal goals with those of the organization, so that both may be accomplished. Staff development is usually the first major concern of administrators who must recruit, select, and orient teachers of adults.

Harris and Bessent (1969) define staff development as one of several planned organizational change strategies available to administrators. As such, it is a goal-directed activity designed to bring about changes in people rather than in rules, structures, policies, or the physical environment.

The goals of staff development should be grounded in the philosophy and goals of continuing education in general and in the specific needs and purposes of the particular continuing education agency. The goals of staff development should reflect the basic educational needs of the instructional staff.

A staff development program that meets institutional goals and instructional needs will most likely include the components of initial orientation and in-service education.

Initial Orientation of New Staff

Orientation has at least two important purposes. The first is to provide introductory instruction for new staff members so that they can quickly perceive the policies, procedures, and daily related routines of their new assignments. More subtle, however, is the need to help the new teacher become aware of the roles of his or her new colleagues, to perceive his or her own role within this new situation, and to decide how he or she can contribute effectively to the organization's goals.

The specific content of orientation programs will vary according to the needs of each agency. Often administrators can use the orientation phase to build a psychosocial climate of support and trust for the new staff person. It is important not only for them to see how and why certain things are done in certain ways, but also to be encouraged to try new procedures or methods. New teachers may be slightly bewildered as they begin their new jobs. There is a fine line between overloading them with many details and providing them with the essential information they need immediately to begin teaching. Some common elements found in most orientation programs are discussed below.

Organizational Goals and Structure. Goals, organizational charts, and institutional expectations are usually shared at this time. It is quite helpful for new staff members to have either a printed handbook or a loose-leaf notebook that contains this important information about the institution. Mimeographed handouts can be added to the notebooks as needed in the future.

Institutional Policies and Rules. The handbook or notebook should also contain information about the policies and procedures necessary for daily teaching activities. New teachers should be familiar with payroll and personnel policies, including personnel contract agreements, payroll policy explanations, pay check disbursement procedures, and whom to contact if payroll errors occur.

Most continuing education agencies must keep accurate attendance records for their own use and for reporting to the parent organization and sometimes to a government agency. Registration procedures and enrollment and reporting forms should be explained to new teachers during orientation.

The new teacher should have a calendar showing dates that may affect the teaching schedule, such as the beginning and ending of courses, holidays, when grades are due, and commencement ceremonies.

New teachers should be introduced to the evaluation policies and expectations of the agency. Are grades to be assigned? Are they based on the normal curve of probability? Are competency-based criteria used? What should be the minimal level of acceptable performance before a student completes the course? Are pass-fail options available? Can teachers contract with students for specific grades?

Does the agency provide for multiple copies of course materials? What kinds of duplication are available—offset, dry copy, mimeograph, ditto, or xerox copying? What is the amount of time required for using these services? How and where are the services requested?

Does the agency have audiovisual equipment? How is it requested? Does the teacher pick it up or is there a delivery service? Is there a media specialist who can help new teachers design items such as 35mm slides, overhead transparencies, color lifts, and flannelgraphs appropriate to the teacher's special topic area? Are funds available for new teachers to purchase commercial audiovisual packages?

New teachers need to know if an on-site bookstore exists and when it is open. They need to know how to order books and other supplies. What are the time lines for ordering and stocking required texts? If an on-site bookstore does not exist, are there commercial bookstores that handle such requests?

Some agencies have procedures of accounting for long-distance calls related to courses that are taught. Such reporting requirements should be clarified at the outset.

Most agencies have specific procedures and budget allocations for courses. Some courses may be taught with private or governmental grant support. These funds are kept separate for auditing purposes. Teachers need to know whether or not they are teaching under a grant and what procedures they must follow.

Practical Classroom Management Suggestions. Much of what teachers want to know focuses on classroom management strategies. While it is true that "an old head cannot be put on new shoulders," it is equally true that new teachers can learn many practical tips from experienced teachers. Administrators might find it useful to invite some effective teachers of adults to an orientation meeting to serve as resource persons. A number of common and relevant questions could be asked and views shared in a discussion period. For example, one might explore the issue of the late enrollee who misses a large portion of the first evening's presentation. How does the effective teacher integrate that person into a group with other participants?

Another activity might be to identify several "ice-breaker" activities that are appropriate for adult learners during the first session. Another useful topic would be a discussion on whether or not adults wish to be tested or if there are other ways teachers can assess students' progress.

Establishing Classroom Climate. More adult learners are won or lost because of the way the first session is conducted than for any other reason. This is particularly true when the learners have been away from formal education for some time. These adults often require some psychological support to bolster their confidence and assure them that the teacher and the agency will do everything possible to make their learning an exciting adventure.

Orientation should help the new teacher focus on techniques that set an appropriate mood for the first session. One useful device is to ask the learners to discuss their backgrounds and reasons for taking the course. This often reveals the common anxieties, goals, experiences, and interests of the participants. Often new friendships develop beyond the classroom itself.

The new teacher of adults should learn during orientation that the first session is more critical than any other during the course or workshop. How these adults are treated as they enter the room—with a smile or a frown, with excitement or a flat monotone in the teacher's voice, with an air of informality or impersonal formality—in large measure sets the learning tone for the rest of the program.

Anticipating and Preventing Common Problems. Systematic planning is the key here. Every agency has cycles when everyone is busy, followed by slack periods. The busy periods should be planned for carefully. For example, for evening credit courses, the busy periods are usually the weeks before and after instruction begins. Is there sufficient classroom space? Have some courses been canceled? If so, can students get into other courses they want? Are textbooks in? Are any courses too large for their assigned rooms? Are students going through drop and add? Do new teachers know the procedures for helping new students get enrolled? Are class syllabi and handout materials ready for the first session?

Another predictably busy period for a credit course is at midterm. Are tests required? Do teachers mark and score their exams? Are computer scoring services available? Must midterm grades be submitted to the parent organization?

Finally, the end of the semester is often busy too. In addition to administering and evaluating any final tests, reading papers, and assessing individual and group projects, teachers are often requested to write letters of reference for students and to provide advice on future course work. Administrators and instructional supervisors can do much to ease the pressure for teachers during these cyclical periods by planning carefully for them during less busy periods.

In-Service Education

The supervisor also needs to attend to a sequence of systematically planned activities for the instructional improvement of experienced teaching faculty and instructional support staff in an agency. Because of their supporting role in the teaching-learning process, it is useful to include the members of the instructional support staff in in-service activities. There are several important reasons why on-going in-service education is required. First, in those agencies which employ part-time staff from the community in special teaching areas (such as real estate, personal finances, and estate planning), this may be the teachers' only contact with adult education theory and practice. Second, it is important for all teachers to be aware of and able to use a new curriculum and new methods and techniques. Third, if in-service education is designed to equip teachers to perform at their highest level of achievement, then there should be an immediate transfer from the in-service education to the teacher's own work with adult learners.

There are at least four general instructional goals inherent in each in-service activity. First, teachers must become familiar with the policies and practices that will enable them to perform effectively. Second, they must develop or enhance their specific proficiencies, usually through hands-on experiential activities. Third, they must assess their personal value systems and compare them with those of the agency. Fourth, they must share and compare their professional insights with those of other teachers.

An exhaustive list of content or topics cannot be provided here, because the particular educational needs of the instructional staff in each instance dictates what should be presented. This is especially true when new part-time teachers come from a variety of organizations in a community and have had little if any preparation for teaching adults. Even in agencies that are made up mainly of school or college teachers, administrators should remember that these teachers have much to learn about teaching adults. Hence, the needs of the teachers of adults should set the content of an in-service education program. Numerous techniques are available for assessing the educational needs and interests of the teachers and instructional support staff.

A review of previous in-service education programs for teachers of adults reveals some common topics. The following subject areas and brief descriptions are intended to suggest topics that may be appropriate.

Institutional Policies and Administrative Procedures. Most teachers want to know specific policy information and administrative procedures basic to the success of their instruction. This is an area that helps build faculty rapport. If these topics have been dealt with effectively in an orientation program, there may be little need to focus on them in in-service activities, other than to present new policies and procedures and to discuss the teacher's questions.

The Psychology of the Adult Learner. The 1960s and the 1970s witnessed some excellent scholarly contributions to our understanding of adult learners. Teachers of adults would gain much insight from reading and discussing chapters 1 to 6 of Kidd's (1973) book on how adults learn. Miller (1964) has provided a relevant book on teaching and learning in adult education. Knox (1977) has summarized the salient research findings on adult development and learning. Other authors have studied stages of adult development (see Havighurst, 1952; Levinson, 1978; Sheehy, 1976). Merriam (1979) has reviewed the research on middle age.

A significant school of thought, proposed by Malcolm Knowles (1970; 1973), stresses differences between the ways in which children and adults should be taught. Knowles (1970, pp. 38–40) uses the term *andragogy* as opposed to *pedagogy* and defines it as the art and science of helping adults learn how to learn. His theory of teaching adults is based on four major psychological assumptions about the nature of adults. First, the maturing, growing adult learner desires to move from a passive-dependent to a self-directing, proactive learner. Second, the adult is a rich treasure chest of experiences that should be used as a resource for learning. Third, the adult's readiness to learn is closely related to his or her ever-changing life roles and developmental tasks. And fourth, the adult learner's time perspective changes from one of postponed application to one of immediate application of learning to life-centered problems.

Techniques for Teaching Adults. Many techniques that work well for teaching children are also appropriate for teaching adults. There are, however, techniques that have been developed specifically for and tested with adult learners. These techniques stress the active participatory experience of adults in the learning situation. Craig (1976) provides an excellent source that describes many of these techniques.

Proficiency in the use of large- and small-group discussion methods helps the teachers who wish to use the talents of adult learners in their courses. How a teacher conducts an individual class session varies from person to person. Continuing education teachers stress learner participation as much as possible, and some strategy that actively engages the learner is desired. Student reports, group presentations, experiential or hands-on activities, educational games, group problem solving, consensus building, team building, and values clarification all draw extensively on the adult's experiences. Often combinations of these activities enliven individual class sessions, and learners feel a sense of excitement as they learn together. One excellent resource in this area is the book by Bergevin, Morris, and Smith (1963) on various group procedures, which outlines the roles and responsibilities of group members.

Role playing and related simulation techniques can be used to help adult learners experience and empathize with the attitudes, values, and feelings that arise in situations of high emotion or conflict.

Using Teaching Aids. Audiovisual aids can enrich and enliven lectures, stimulate a student's desire to learn, help hold attention, encourage greater acquisition and longer retention of information, and make the learning available to wider adult audiences. Teachers may need to acquire expertise with nonprojected visual aids (including pictorial aids, blackboards, flannelgraphs, and magnetic boards), projectors (including opaque, slide, film strip, overhead, single film loop, and 16mm film), closed circuit TV, and electronic videorecording units. Teachers also may need assistance in preparing teacher-made aids and in choosing commercial projected and nonprojected materials.

Clearly, then, teachers should have the opportunity to learn the proper and effective use of each teaching aid and its advantages and disadvantages. Dale (1956) has provided a useful reference in this area.

Identifying and Writing Instructional Objectives. The 1970s saw a clearer understanding of the role of educational objectives in contributing to adult learning in a variety of educational settings. Using the rationale behind military training, more and more teachers of adults adopted the strategy of specifying the behaviors expected of adult learners on completion of a course of study. In what types of performance should the student be able to engage by the end of the course? What factual questions should he or she be able to answer? What personal characteristics of the learner ought to be affected? These and similar questions help learners know exactly what the expectations are, where they are going in the course, and where they are at any moment in their journey toward their specific destination. This instructional strategy is succinctly described in Mager's well-known book, *Preparing Instructional Objectives* (1962).

Developing and Organizing Individual Courses. Teachers are often puzzled about how to organize (or reorganize) and teach a course. This issue is partly answered by the nature of the content of the course and by the nature of the students.

Survey courses covering materials relatively unfamiliar to most of the adult learners might call for at least two strategies. First, the instructor can follow the chapter topics of a textbook. This assumes that the textbook author has done a good job of selecting and sequencing the content in ways that are meaningful to the students. This is not always the case, however. Second, the instructor can develop his or her own organizational approach, in which he or she lays out the topics and then selectively assigns various learning experiences, which could include readings from several texts that support this approach. This strategy allows great flexibility for the instructor to pull together relevant resource materials.

Suppose, however, that this is an advanced course in which many learners already possess some degree of knowledge. Perhaps the best strategy is to use the psychological approach in which the students are asked to raise questions about issues that still puzzle them. Then the course can be organized around the specific interests of the learners in the course. In this instance the course syllabus cannot be developed until after the first session.

Regardless of the strategy used, a course syllabus should contain several important sections. First, a brief general overview of the course should be presented. Second, specific behavioral learning objectives should be listed so that the learners know what skills, knowledge, and attitudes can be acquired during the course. Third, a list of the topics to be covered should be provided, along with their presentation dates. A bibliographic source list for each topic area should be given so that all learners can prepare for the class presentation and discussion. Fourth, any evaluation expectations should be explained. This should include statements regarding the value and weight of any tests, class reports, projects, class participation, and class attendance.

Evaluation. Every course needs to have evaluation built into it to assess student and teacher performance. A teacher needs proficiency in how to assess student learning, in how to identify any weaknesses in teaching so they may be corrected, and in how to make changes for course improvement. Accordingly, many teachers devise midcourse rating scales for learners to identify needed course corrections in an anonymous manner. Some more confident teachers may use classroom discussion to achieve the same purposes.

End-of-course evaluations are also helpful to the students and the teachers. One approach is for teachers and students to discuss how well specific course objectives were met and other aspects of the course that could be improved. What objectives were not met? Were some unrealistic? Should others be added? Was too much time spent on one or two sections to the exclusion of others?

In addition to this open-ended discussion, many agencies require anonymous student evaluations. The results of these evaluations may be used to compare courses and instructors throughout the agency. Instructors will need to be aware of such policies, of how the evaluations are implemented, and of how the results will be used.

In-Service Education Advisory Committees

Continuing education supervisors and administrators have long used advisory committees of teachers to assist in assessing the needs of the instructional staff and in planning the content of in-service education. In continuing education it is important to involve the learners themselves in assessing their educational needs and in planning programs to meet those needs, because, first, a democratic environment is created that supports the belief that people can grow and change and that everyone is unique and worthwhile. Second, learner involvement allows for the development of subcommittees to carry out various in-service responsibilities so that no one is overworked throughout the year. These subcommittees can draw on both experienced and new faculty to assess the need for and interest in new offerings in continuing education and their respective subject areas, to recruit resource specialists (both from within their own instructional staff and from external consultants), and to encourage learning of a high quality. And third, participatory planning stresses the belief that adults, when given the chance, can rationally plan and will take on the responsibility to define their own needs, set their own goals, and help achieve these goals without having to rely on "outside experts" to tell them what they need to know.

Thus the representative advisory committee helps turn teachers' questions back on themselves so that they accept some responsibility for their learning. Hopefully the teacher of adults then carries that participatory model into the classroom with his or her adult learners.

Composition of Advisory Committees. How many persons should serve on an advisory committee? There is no fixed answer, of course, but most administrators find that a small group of six to eight persons, representative of the instructional staff, should be invited to serve. This small number permits maximum interaction and sharing of vital information and ideas.

Responsibilities of Advisory Committees. An advisory and planning committee has a number of responsibilities crucial to the success of a staff development program.

The committee should assist in the development of a statement of the philosophy, goals, and objectives of the in-service program. Using the stated purposes of their institution, agency, or organization, the committee should decide how the in-service program will prepare teachers of adults to achieve the organization's goals.

It should help develop plans for surveying the needs and interests of the instructional staff and share in the specific tasks involved in carrying out these plans, and it should help establish annual priorities among the many needs, interests, and problems that surface during the needs assessment.

Within the limits of its delegated authority the committee should help establish policies governing the in-service program. For example, it should address the questions of when and where the activities will occur and the issue of teacher compensation.

It should help formulate both the short-term and the long-term goals of the total annual in-service program. It can interpret the future needs of the in-service program to agency administrators. In doing this, the advisory committee has the chance to influence policy and decision makers to enhance their view of in-service education from a mere luxury to one of necessity for organizational effectiveness and growth. It can also help evaluate the in-service education program in terms of the goals met and further goals to be achieved.

Policy Issues Connected With In-Service Education

When should in-service education be held? How often? How much time should be given to it? Should teachers receive some compensation for their time and effort? These questions are especially important to part-time faculty whose main loyalty is to their full-time jobs, to their families, and to their avocational pursuits.

Part-time teachers may resist attending sessions scheduled for evenings when their courses are not held, on weekends, or during vacation periods. This question is inextricably related to the compensation issue. If the agency expects in-service education to be taken seriously, it must support the notion that learning how to be a better teacher is an important part of the job assignment. There are very persuasive reasons for compensating teachers for attending in-service sessions. Precedence for this practice is well established for staff in the Cooperative Extension Service, and for teachers in public schools, community colleges, and vocational-technical schools.

The question of how much and how often training should be held does not have a satisfactory answer. Although there is no hard and fast rule concerning how much in-service education is necessary, there should be a definite organizational commitment to staff development and to compensating teachers of adults who attend in-service education activities.

In the late 1960s the National Education Association recommended that a minimum requirement of ten hours of in-service education in methods of teaching adults be offered during the school year at no cost to the teachers, that teachers should receive their regular rate of pay, and that the program should be scheduled during the regular hours of the continuing education program (Luke and Ulmer, 1971). More recently, federal and state agencies that conduct in-service education for employees have suggested a minimum of forty hours of in-service education a year for their trainers. This training may be given by individual agencies or by the United States Civil Service Commission.

Design Models for Staff Development Activities

Numerous models exist that can help administrators plan systematically for in-service education. The value of using any model is that it helps planners make decisions, in a step-by-step manner, about strategies for a successful program.

The following planning models from adult and continuing education engage adult learners (in this instance, the instructional staff) in examining their own needs and in helping plan, conduct, and evaluate programs to meet these needs. The major advantage of program planning models developed by continuing educators is that they assume a high degree of responsibility for learning on the part of the adult learner. That is, they operate on the assumption that adults can and will be self-directing and proactive learners when given the opportunity.

Knox (1971) developed a model for the in-service education of adult basic education instructional staff that uses the concept of need appraisal as a starting point for program development. His model can be described as a discrepancy model, in which the desired excellent performances of teachers (as revealed by research) are compared and contrasted with the current performances of the instructional staff. The gap between the two is the area of educational need, and a program is designed to close the gap.

Knox's model uses five steps: appraising the situation by examining the local symptoms of the needed in-service education; identifying needs by comparing the current performances of teachers with those of known outstanding teachers; selecting the needs that have become clear; developing the program plan with special attention to specifying objectives, intended input, transactions, outcomes, and evaluation procedures; and conducting the program.

Three advantages of Knox's model are the careful attention to detail, the validation of the observed needs of teachers of a local agency against those reported by other agencies, and the strong emphasis on evaluation.

Houle (1972) developed a fundamental system of educational design consisting of the following eight components of a successful program: a possible educational activity is identified; a decision is made to proceed; objectives are identified and refined; a suitable format is designed (which includes the management of learning strategies and learning options); the format is fitted into larger patterns of life (that is, the learner's personal life-styles are shaped to meet the needs of the educational program); the plan is put into effect; the results are measured and appraised; and the situation is reexamined in terms of the possibility of a new educational activity.

Londoner (1972) developed an administrative planning model for continuing education based on the systems approach to or network-based models of administrative decision making. It is primarily an input-throughput-output model similar to those used in business for planning activities. The model uses eight steps, depicted in a flow chart design with feedback loops indicating that it is both cyclical and linear. The eight steps are: the statement of the identified needs and problems; the development of measurable objectives to meet the identified needs and problems; a definition of the system constraints, including a statement of program feasibility in light of the constraints; the development of alternatives to achieve the objectives; analysis and selection of each alternative in light of the system constraints and specific criteria, including selection of the best alternative; the development and pilot implementation of the best alternative; feedback and modification for program refinement; and evaluation (determining if the program is achieving its intended objectives). A major advantage of this model is its ability to manage many of the details that must be considered in a long-term program.

Knowles' (1970) andragogical model of program development purposely involves the adult learners in the planning process so that they become responsible for their own learning. An advisory and planning committee can easily use this model for planning, conducting, and evaluating their in-service education program. It employs seven steps: establishing a climate conducive to learning, creating a structure for mutual planning, diagnosing the needs for learning, formulating program purposes and objectives, designing a pattern of learning experiences, conducting the learning activities, and rediagnosing the learner's needs.

Ingalls (1973) field-tested the andragogical model of staff development for the Department of Health, Education, and Welfare and found it suitable for in-service education in terms of personal self-development and for industrial organizational development programs. Davis and McCallon (1975) adapted the andragogical model to planning, conducting, and evaluating workshops. Their book is designed to help administrators carry out systematically all the essential tasks for planning successful workshops.

Whichever model an administrator decides to use, there are several elements common to all. First, each is based on the assumption that adult learners (in this instance, members of the instructional staff) are capable of identifying their own needs, and helping conduct and evaluate their own learning. Second, each model presupposes that sufficient time will be spent on planning each component so that the model can evolve soundly—thus assuring a successful program. And finally, each model is basically cyclical in nature. Each step assumes a flow forward and backward to and from each element, so that the needs of the learners can be met. This permits a checking and rechecking of each element in the program design for possible modifications to improve the in-service education activity.

Summary

I have examined a number of factors that affect staff development activities for teachers of adults. Systematic planning by administrators is essential in order to meet the educational needs of their instructional staff. Effective in-service education begins with a sound orientation program that introduces teachers of adults to organizational goals, policies, and structure and helps build a spirit of cooperation and enthusiasm, and continues with programs developed by administrative personnel and advisory committee members working in conjunction.

References

Bergevin, P., Morris, D. M., and Smith, R. M. *Adult Education Procedures: A Handbook of Tested Patterns for Effective Participation.* New York: Seabury Press, 1963.

Craig, R. L. *Training and Development Handbook.* (2nd ed.) New York: McGraw-Hill, 1976.

Dale, E. *Audiovisual Methods in Teaching.* (3rd ed.) New York: Dryden Press, 1956.

Davis, L. N., and McCallon, E. *Planning, Conducting, and Evaluating Workshops.* Austin, Tex.: Learning Concepts, 1975.

Harris, B. M., and Bessent, W. *In-Service Education: A Guide to Better Practice.* Englewood Cliffs, N.J.: Prentice-Hall, 1969.

Havighurst, R. J. *Developmental Tasks and Aging.* New York: McKay, 1952.

Houle, C. O. *The Design of Education.* San Francisco: Jossey-Bass, 1972.

Ingalls, J. D. *A Trainers Guide to Andragogy.* (rev. ed.) Washington, D.C.: U.S. Government Printing Office, 1973.

Kidd, J. R. *How Adults Learn.* (rev. ed.) New York: Association Press, 1973.

Knowles, M. S. *The Modern Practice of Adult Education: Andragogy Versus Pedagogy.* New York: Associated Press, 1970.

Knowles, M. S. *The Adult Learner: A Neglected Species.* Houston, Tex.: Gulf Publishing Co., 1973.

Knox, A. B. *In-Service Education in Adult Basic Education.* Tallahassee: Research Information Processing Center, Department of Adult Education, Florida State University, 1971.

Knox, A. B. *Adult Development and Learning.* San Francisco: Jossey-Bass, 1977.

Levinson, D. J. *The Seasons of a Man's Life.* New York: Knopf, 1978.

Londoner, C. A. "The Systems Approach as an Administrative and Program Planning Tool for Continuing Education." *Educational Technology,* 1972, *12* (8), 24-31.

Luke, R., and Ulmer, C. *How to Train Teachers to Train Adults.* Englewood Cliffs, N.J.: Prentice-Hall, 1971.

Mager, R. F. *Preparing Instructional Objectives.* Palo Alto, Calif.: Fearon, 1962.

Merriam, S. "Middle Age: A Review of the Research." In A. B. Knox (Ed.), *Programming for Adults Facing Mid-life Change.* San Francisco: Jossey-Bass, 1979.
Miller, L. *Teaching and Learning in Adult Education.* New York: Macmillan, 1964.
Sheehy, G. *Passages: Predictable Crises of Adult Life.* New York: Dutton, 1976.

Carroll A. Londoner is associate professor of adult education and the associate director of the adult education program, Virginia Commonwealth University.

A visit? Why me? Is something wrong with my teaching?

Supervision and Monitoring

Lloyd L. Brumfield
Doris P. Nesbit

For years supervision has been viewed by educators as a mixed blessing. On the one hand, it can be considered an honor to be selected for visitation. Teachers seem to adjust to having visitors in their classrooms. In fact, most teachers seem to enjoy being able to "show off" and "let the ham in them" really show.

On the other hand, as soon as notice is given that the supervisor is coming, questions begin to be verbalized. Why me? What do they want in my classroom? What am I expected to do? What are they looking for? What have I done or not done?

Supervising Adult Teachers

What accounts for these differing attitudes toward supervision on the part of continuing education teachers? The answer cannot be simple, because of the variety of personal qualities involved (such as a teacher's need for autonomy or attitude toward authority) and the nature of a teacher's previous experience with being supervised. Teachers who were prepared for elementary or secondary teaching have had several people in a supervisory capacity evaluate their performance for grading purposes. But some postsecondary education teachers may be socialized to believe that supervision is an infringement of academic freedom (Wilson and others, 1969).

Teachers who regard supervision in a positive light do not feel threatened by the process. Rather, they perceive supervision as a form of consultation that helps them improve, or as a way of recognizing good performance.

The majority of teachers, however, probably views supervision with skepticism and anxiety. Supervision, to them, is evaluation, the results of which are used for sorting teachers into grade categories or for emphasizing what is wrong with their classroom situations (such as methods, lesson plans, discipline, innovations, and attitudes). Supervision is seen, all too often, as "snoopervision."

A Definition of Supervision. Supervisors do not have to be "snoopies," but a supervisor may have to overcome the feeling that he or she is a central office inspector. We prefer Webster's definition of a supervisor as "an administrative officer of a school (or educational) system who assists a teacher in curriculum planning and method of instruction or in the teaching of a special subject." To supervise is "to look over accomplishments" in order to direct or coordinate. "Supervision is a service activity that exists to help teachers do their job better" (Campbell, Corbally, and Ramseyer, 1962, p. 295). Van Dersal (1968, p. 25) defines supervision as "the art of working with a group over whom authority is exercised in such a way as to achieve their greatest combined effectiveness in getting work done." The purpose of all supervision is to improve the services of the department (in this instance, the teaching process), and the key criterion of effective supervision is the extent to which it inspires the teacher or leader to want to do a better job (Burrichter and Gardner, 1979; Rauch, 1972; Shaw, 1969).

The Role of Supervision. The prime responsibility of a supervisor is that of a helping agent. The current literature on supervision stresses such topics as delegation of authority and responsibility, job enlargement and job enrichment, participatory decision making, and management by objectives. The challenge for a supervisor, according to Haimann and Hilgert (1972), is to develop an approach that will give people more responsibility, a sense of achievement, participation, recognition, and a chance and desire to advance. Not only must the supervisor be knowledgeable about the organizational philosophy and mission and the teaching-learning process, he or she must be able to work with people to help them become more effective teachers. Understanding theories of and acquiring proficiency in human relations, organization, communications, power, influence, leadership, and teaching underlie the power of the helping relationship.

Understanding Why People Behave As They Do

The study of values and why people behave as they do has become a major interest of supervisory personnel. Kubie (1958, p. 526) concluded that "the clinical fact which is already evident is that once a central emotional position is established early in life, it becomes the affective position to which that individual will automatically return for the rest of his days."

Hierarchy of Needs. Much has been said about Maslow's (1954) hierarchy of needs. Maslow developed the concept that there are five levels of psychological needs that seem to be arranged in a hierarchical order in which each is satisfied or fulfilled. Initially, physiological (or physical survival) needs have the highest strength until they are somewhat satisfied. The other categories of needs that become important as motivators of behavior when the preceding levels are met are safety or security needs, social or affiliation needs, esteem or recognition needs, and self-actualization needs. Supervisors should understand how they can help teachers meet some of those needs and how, in turn, teachers can help them fulfill their needs.

Theory X-Theory Y. This classic theory, developed by McGregor (1960), also enables supervisors to examine their assumptions about human nature and human motivation. McGregor concluded that different management and supervisory styles develop from the different assumptions held. One view, Theory X, of how to manage people assumes that people are lazy, prefer to be directed, dislike work, are motivated primarily by money and safety, and have little capacity for problem solving. Thus supervisors should control, direct, and closely supervise people. Theory Y holds that people find work a source of satisfaction under favorable conditions, want and seek responsibility, are motivated by all five levels of Maslow's psychological needs, and are capable of self-direction and creative problem solving. The Theory Y supervisor allows teachers to progressively assume more and more self-control of their work and to arrange for people to work together for the success of the organization.

Motivator-Hygiene Theory. Studies by Herzberg, Mausner, and Snydermann (1959) have resulted in the motivator-hygiene theory of a person's attitude toward a job. Van Dersal (1968, p. 76) concludes that the evidence is "now overwhelming that the theory is essentially correct." Herzberg and his associates found that people identified five factors that made them feel good about their jobs—a sense of achievement, recognition for good work, interesting and challenging work, opportunities for responsibility, and advancement. People who were unhappy about their jobs cited different factors—unfair or harmful policies and administration, incompetent or unfair supervision, unfair handling of salaries, unsatisfying relationships with the supervisor, and poor or inconvenient working conditions. The "satisfier" and "dissatisfier" factors were also found to operate more or less independently of each other and in different directions.

Central Value Positions. Jelinek (1978) has theorized that there are three basic central value positions or ego states that children develop, which affect a person for the rest of his or her life. Those central value positions are that of a trainee ego state, a trainer ego state, and a teacher-learner ego state.

In the trainee ego state a person feels powerless and at the mercy of others. The child was manipulated, rewarded, and punished by the trainer and learned to accept passively the judgments and reactions of others. "Submission to authority, desire for a strong leader to tell in behavioristic terms what to do, when to do it, how to do it, and even how to feel about it, all characterize [this] ego state" (Jelinek, 1978, p. 188). The supervisor should look for submissiveness, obedience, and respect in identifying teachers whose central value position can be characterized as that of a trainee.

A trainer ego state is developed when the person lives under a system of rigid restraint and his or her behavior is essentially copied from authority figures. There is a sadistic component to this person; he or she feels the necessity to find another person to "take it out on" and gets extremely annoyed if someone appears to be getting away with something. The behavior and consequences of a supervisor whose value position is the trainer ego state are important because of the amount of power that a supervisor may have in everyday situations. The continuous forcing of responses to desired outcomes can condition people into submissive behavior and into being easily manipulated. The trainer ego state supervisor may also create conflict situations. The teacher may have a different idea or value; therefore conflict occurs because no compromise is possible on the two viewpoints. Dehumanization may also occur if the trainee fails to see that the supervision or training efforts contradict reality. When a supervisor operating in the trainer ego state is able to completely dominate and manipulate another person, forms of exploitation and personal abuse are developed.

The value position for which a supervisor should strive is the teacher-learner ego state. Here the attitude is that everyone is a person and no one is an object. This person uses modes of inquiry and problem solving in day-to-day experiences. The teacher-learner ego state produces an interpersonal relationship in which power is shared among supervisors, teachers, and students. Didactic narration turns to communication; thinking replaces unquestioning acceptance of information; unity of goals and purpose develop between supervisor, teacher and students; and teachers and supervisors become colleagues rather than superior and subordinate.

Many other theories and studies pertaining to motivation and leadership are found in the literature. For summaries of selected books and articles relevant to supervision, the interested reader should consult Van Dersal (1968) and Hersey and Blanchard (1972).

Conditioning or Andragogy?

The Pavlovian idea that we are conditioned to respond as a fundamental unit of habit has been expanded by Holt (1931) to describe a psychology of learning based solely on the principles of conditioning.

Recent writers (Skinner, 1971; Jelinek, 1978) caution that external stimuli can condition human beings to lose their freedom for infinite individuality and to choose activities that lead to submissiveness rather than self-actualization.

Knowles (1973) has suggested some assumptions about adult learners that support a facilitator rather than a manipulator role for teachers of adults. The four basic assumptions about adult learners posited by Knowles are: adults view themselves as independent rather than dependent people, capable of making decisions for themselves; adults have accumulated vast quantities of experience of differing kinds; adults' readiness to learn is related more to social roles and developmental tasks than to biological changes and tasks; and adults are oriented to problem solving in the present rather than acquisition of content for future use. In addition, the concept of andragogy recognizes the need for self-direction of adult learners. Among the implications for continuing education are that life experiences and involving adult learners in the planning process need to be considered when offering learning activities for adults.

In *A Trainer's Guide to Andragogy*, Ingalls and Arceri (1972) propose that the following conditions should be present when teaching adults: reciprocity in the teaching-learning transaction, multicommunication shared by all, learners grouped according to interest, and problem-finding and problem-solving teams. Just as a teacher's role in the andragogical process is that of a facilitator rather than a sole manager of content, so the supervisor can assume a similar posture in dealing with learning situations for teachers. What better place to begin to demonstrate techniques for teachers of adults than in the supervision-teaching relationship?

The theory and research findings pertaining to motivation, psychological needs, the use of power in human relationships, and andragogy point to the need to involve the teacher in the supervisory process. Human organizations require human agents of change (Harris, 1975).

Areas of Practical Application

Classroom Management and Organization. Continuing education administrators should provide teachers with a manual that contains the agency's philosophy, regulations, and course offerings and descriptions to enhance the teacher's management and organization of the classroom. Otherwise a supervisor may have to assist the inexperienced teacher of adults to understand the basic procedures of organizing and managing a classroom. Such understanding should not be assumed. Many full-time teachers in schools or colleges teach part-time in the continuing education program. Yet some otherwise proficient teachers fail to provide for proper ventilation in the classroom. A checklist of classroom management responsibilities would include the following: adjusting the classroom environment to minimize outside distractions (continuing education programs often have much traffic in the halls); assuring proper lighting, ventilation, and heating (needs vary for different ages); arranging seats so that interaction may be experienced by adult learners and teachers; using visuals or aids that provide for a visibility level adequate for adults; planning and previewing supplemental material for appropriateness for adults; preparing an adequate number of copies of materials for distribution; alloting equitable time for each adult learner; allowing and encouraging adult learners to express themselves; maintaining an adequate stock of material and supplies in the classroom (often a problem because of sharing rooms with day school teachers); observing time limits for breaks; and beginning and ending instruction promptly at the scheduled times (usually there is no bell system).

Instructional Techniques. Another area where the supervisor can assist the teacher, and particularly the new teacher, is that of instructional techniques. A class break, a personal conference, or an in-service education program would be good opportunities for the supervisor to suggest or discuss teaching techniques to use with adults. Some common suggestions are: show enthusiasm during class activities; share with the class the course outlines and plans for meeting the objectives of the course; have a teaching plan available for each session; review previously learned material at the beginning of each class; present the objectives for each new lesson to the class; summarize the lesson and preview the next session before dismissal; plan for the participation of adult students in the class activities; moderate discussions so that class members do not digress from the topic; treat adults as adults; provide a brief but relevant exercise while students wait for class to begin; vary activities so as not to do the same activity too long; use guest speakers, films, demonstrations, and displays to vary class activities; provide opportunity for students to work at different levels; give attention to each adult in some way during the lesson; provide adults with opportunities to relate their experiences as part of the learning in the classroom; answer questions as a learning technique; use small groups to enable students to work at various levels; use vocabulary building as part of class work; reinforce often the areas covered for internalization of the concepts; and vary the method of evaluation. Additions to these points should be made by the supervisor according to visible signs of need.

Teacher Evaluation. Supervisors can involve teachers in the evaluation process through self-evaluation efforts. Self-evaluation questions such as the following can be used to help improve teaching:
- How clearly do I present my subject matter?
- How well do I adjust to the level of comprehension of the adult students?
- How much am I learning from the students in the class?
- How well am I prepared for class meetings?

- Do I require much original thinking of the students?
- Are student questions related to the lesson being studied?
- How interesting do I make the material?
- How well do I seem to know my subject?
- How tolerant am I of the opinions of others?
- How do I give constructive criticism and make corrections?
- How is my sense of humor?
- How free am I from annoying personal peculiarities and mannerisms?
- What is the feeling between me and the students?
- Do I encourage class discussion by the students?
- Do I ever use sarcasm and ridicule as a disciplinary measure?
- Do I display courtesy and self-control?
- How much do I enjoy teaching?
- Do I practice what I preach?
- Do I give assignments clearly?
- Are the assigned readings valuable?
- Is class time well spent?
- How valuable and meaty is the content of my course?
- Are grading policies fair?
- Do I really enjoy working with adults and helping them learn?
- Have I studied and reflected on the need for adult education?
- Am I aware of individual differences among adult students and how these affect my relationships with them?
- Have I conscientiously sought to identify individual differences in my class group?
- Am I striving to become more of a leader and a learner in my class and less of a formal instructor?
- Am I bringing in qualified people who make contributions toward group objectives?
- Do I know what equipment is available and am I using it to the best advantage?
- Am I making use of libraries, museums, public agencies, civic organizations, and news media?
- Am I using information from today's meeting in preparation for tomorrow's?
- Am I allowing my leadership to be improved by group evaluation?
- Have I established good relations with other members of the staff and am I familiar with their programs?

Student Retention and Recruitment. Adult students are, of course, not required to enroll. Usually adults enroll because they have a personal interest in learning or a psychological need to do so. A continuing education activity has to compete with other leisure time activities such as television and sports. Nor is the spirit of lifelong learning always responded to by taking a course. Therefore, attraction and retention of participants are important objectives, and teachers can help.

Supervisors can distribute information to potential participants about the course offerings. In large agencies the supervisor can help form a coalition among local centers and avoid needless duplication so that classes can meet minimum enrollments.

The supervisor can help teachers learn promotional techniques. With such assistance many teachers are willing to help. Sometimes just knowing how and where to promote a new course is sufficient, and a supervisor can readily provide this information.

In-service Education. Although in-service education is covered in greater detail in another chapter, brief mention is made here of the supervisory role in in-service education. Continuing education agencies usually operate with part-time teachers. This makes the provision of in-service education difficult. For example, full-time public school teachers may utilize their time after school for planning instead of participating in an in-service education activity related to their part-time continuing education teaching. The teacher contract should be consulted before scheduling in-service sessions for continuing education teachers.

Workshops on Saturdays, in the past, have not been popular. In our experience, more interest has been shown in Saturday offerings during the past few years. This could be due to the use of needs assessment to determine what training should be offered, the use of practical applications, and the provision of interesting sessions.

At any rate, a supervisor should conduct a needs assessment to find out what kinds of assistance the teachers feel they need. A sample of an assessment instrument developed in 1978 by Florida Atlantic University is shown in Figure 1 at the end of this chapter. After the tally is taken, the priority of perceived needs can be established. Because everything cannot be offered at once, the priority listing helps the supervisor know where to begin.

The next step is the decision about whom to turn to for the needed instruction—teacher education center, master teacher, continuing education center faculty, or a college or university. Whatever the choice, the supervisor should assist in the planning stages of the offering in order to be responsive to the teachers' expectations.

Teachers should evaluate all in-service workshops and courses. Supervisors should be interested in improving in-service education programs, and numerous techniques and forms can be used to collect teachers' evaluations of the activity and suggestions for improvement.

Selection of Materials. Supervisors can also assist teachers of adults regarding the selection of materials and other resources. This is especially true for part-time teachers who may have limited time for course preparation. It is the responsibility of a supervisor to anticipate the reactions of community members and members of governing boards arising from controversial course content and materials.

Surveys have been developed for reviewing textbooks and supplemental materials. Generally these surveys are lengthy and therefore cannot be included here. By involving teachers in evaluating existing and new materials, a useful "wish list" can be developed for ordering new materials when additional funds become available or when a revised book list is prepared.

Teacher developed materials can be evaluated by asking questions such as the following:
- Do the materials meet the needs of the students?
- Do the materials meet the needs of the teacher?
- Are the materials suitable for an adult's level of interest?
- Are the materials suitable for the reading level of the adult students involved?
- Does the format make it easy to manage?
- Do the materials help participants acquire basic proficiency?

Advisory Councils. The supervisor should involve members of the community in an advisory capacity to keep the supervisor and the teachers informed of the effects of their efforts. The needs of the community and of individual adult learners, when met, can contribute to higher employment rates of those who complete the program and to higher enrollments in the program.

Summary

Supervisors who give of themselves to help those they supervise have no time to snoopervise. The ones who inquire, observe, learn, and experiment in a helpful manner will build a commitment to lifelong learning within themselves, their teachers, and their students.

Figure 1. Adult Education Staff Training Needs Assessment Survey

Purpose.
This instrument is designed to provide program administrators with descriptive information regarding the staff development needs of continuing educators. Information is solicited through an anonymous assessment and compiled on a total program basis. This assessment is not a faculty evaluation. Information gathered through this process will assist program administrators in planning effective staff development activities and providing leadership that will improve the quality of services provided for adult learners.

Directions.
This inventory includes statements related to competencies that have been identified as important by a cross-section of adult educators. For each of items 1 to 30 below,

Figure 1. (continued)

indicate the degree of competence you think you now demonstrate. To assure a valid profile, it is essential that you respond to every item. Mark your responses in the spaces provided next to the statements. Circle the letter that best approximates your perception of your own performance regarding that item. The five degrees of competence are defined as follows:
- a. A slight degree of competency; a definite need for improvement.
- b. Some degree of competency; a need for improvement.
- c. A moderate degree of competency; some need for improvement.
- d. A high degree of competency; may need improvement.
- e. A superior degree of competency; no need for improvement.

Example
TO WHAT DEGREE DO I AS AN ADULT EDUCATOR...
    21. Assess learning needs?   a b ⓒ d e
Meaning: This indicates that you think you have a moderate degree of competency and need some improvement.

Inventory of Adult Educator Competencies
Directions. Circle the appropriate letter for each item according to the preceding directions. Please respond to every item.

TO WHAT DEGREE DO I AS AN ADULT EDUCATOR...

1. Construct learning objectives with measurable outcomes?   a b c d e
2. Interact constructively with adults (approachable, friendly, responsive, and supportive)?   a b c d e
3. Exhibit behavior reflecting a feeling for the dignity and worth of individuals?   a b c d e
4. Understand the role of an adult educator?   a b c d e
5. Provide practical activities for learning?   a b c d e
6. Develop conditions that facilitate learning?   a b c d e
7. Relate effectively to people from a variety of cultural, economic, and occupational backgrounds?   a b c d e
8. Participate in adult education staff development programs?   a b c d e
9. Understand the purposes of adult education within the community?   a b c d e
10. Provide a suitable learning environment?   a b c d e
11. Recognize symptoms of physical deficiencies that may hinder performance?   a b c d e
12. Develop effective working relationships with adult learners?   a b c d e
13. Provide a curriculum that stimulates a high level of aspiration?   a b c d e
14. Explain the role of adult education to both school and community?   a b c d e
15. Use relevant and effective instructional methods?   a b c d e
16. Apply principles of group dynamics?   a b c d e
17. Recognize processes involved in community change?   a b c d e
18. Develop appropriate goals and objectives for adult programs?   a b c d e

Figure 1. (continued)

19.	Communicate in a coherent and logical manner?	a	b	c	d	e
20.	Assist adult learners to develop positive attitudes toward lifelong learning?	a	b	c	d	e
21.	Assess learning needs?	a	b	c	d	e
22.	Identify the major functions of community agencies that serve the social, educational, and training needs of adult learners?	a	b	c	d	e
23.	Identify the needed topics and concepts of each subject taught?	a	b	c	d	e
24.	Demonstrate a commitment to lifelong learning?	a	b	c	d	e
25.	Use performance-based assessment procedures?	a	b	c	d	e
26.	Use community resources in the classroom?	a	b	c	d	e
27.	Assist individual adjustment to the changing nature of our society?	a	b	c	d	e
28.	Promote self-directed learning?	a	b	c	d	e
29.	Encourage the learner's growth through supportive communication?	a	b	c	d	e
30.	Develop and organize a curriculum reflecting the needs of adult learners?	a	b	c	d	e

This model was developed through a research and staff development conducted by Florida Atlantic University under the provision of Section 309 of the Adult Education Act.

References

Burrichter, A. W., and Gardner, D. L. *A Staff Development Model for Adult Educators.* Boca Raton, Fla.: Florida Atlantic University, 1979.
Campbell, R. F., Corbally, J. E. Jr., and Ramseyer, J. A. *Introduction to Educational Administration.* (2nd ed.) Boston: Allyn & Bacon, 1962.
Haimann, T., and Hilgert, F. L. *Supervision: Concepts and Practices of Management.* Cincinnati, Ohio: Southwestern Publishing, 1972.
Harris, B. M. *Supervisory Behavior in Education.* (2nd ed.) Englewood Cliffs, N.J.: Prentice-Hall, 1975.
Hersey, P., and Blanchard, K. H. *Management of Organizational Behavior.* (2nd ed.) Englewood Cliffs, N.J.: Prentice-Hall, 1972.
Herzberg, F., Mausner, B., and Snydermann, B. *The Motivation to Work.* New York: Wiley, 1959.
Holt, E. B. *Animal Drive and the Learning Process.* New York: Henry Holt, 1931.
Ingalls, J. D., and Arceri, J. M. *A Trainer's Guide to Andragogy.* Washington, D.C.: U.S. Government Printing Office, 1972.
Jelinek, J. J. "The Learning of Values." In J. J. Jelinek (Ed.), *Improving the Human Condition.* Washington, D.C.: Association for Supervision and Curriculum Development, 1978, pp. 183-225.
Knowles, M. S. *The Adult Learner: A Neglected Species.* Houston, Tex.: Gulf Publishing Co., 1973.
Kubie, L. S. "The Neurotic Process and the Focus of Physiological and Psychoanalytic Research." *The Journal of Mental Health,* 1958, *104* (435), 518-536.
Maslow, A. H. *Motivation and Personality.* New York: Harper & Row, 1954.
McGregor, D. *The Human Side of Enterprise.* New York: McGraw-Hill, 1960.

Rauch, D. B. (Ed.). *Priorities in Adult Education.* New York: Macmillan, 1972.
Shaw, N. C. (Ed.). *Administration of Continuing Education.* Washington, D.C.: National Association for Public School Adult Education, 1969.
Skinner, B. F. *Beyond Freedom and Dignity.* New York: Knopf, 1971.
Van Dersal, W. R. *The Successful Supervisor.* (rev. ed.) New York: Harper & Row, 1968.
Wilson, L. C., and others. *Sociology of Supervision.* Boston: Allyn & Bacon, 1969.

Lloyd L. Brumfield is supervisor of adult teachers, Dade County School District, Florida.

Doris P. Nesbit is educational specialist, adult education, Dade County School District, Florida.

*A theory of administrative leadership can help avoid
job dissatisfaction and increase motivation on
the part of teachers.*

Effective Administrative Support for Able Teachers

Delight C. Willing

After approval for a program or course has been obtained, the teachers have been selected, and the students have registered, the role of the effective administrator shifts from program manager to educational leader. Appropriate administrative support and leadership must be provided to the able teacher to facilitate quality educational experiences for adult students.

A Theory of Administrative Leadership

Over the past decades, much research has been conducted in the field of leadership. Most of these studies, however, have been carried out by management programs within schools of business, and it is only recently that educators have begun to apply these theories to educational settings. An understanding of some of the findings can be extremely useful to the administrator who wants to provide positive support to the staff for whom he or she is responsible.

Building on the work of Abraham Maslow (1954), Douglas McGregor, (1960), Chris Argyris (1957), and others, Frederick Herzberg (1959) has developed a theory that provides a useful framework for administrative leaders. Herzberg's motivation-hygiene theory asserts that workers have two relatively independent categories of needs that affect how they feel about their jobs. When people feel dissatisfied with their jobs, they are concerned with what Herzberg calls the environment of the job. When they are satisfied with the job, they feel good about the work itself. Herzberg has called the first set of job dissatisfiers "hygiene factors," and the second set of factors "motivators." The two sets of factors can be shown:

Motivators and Hygiene Factors

Hygiene Factors	*Motivators*
Environment	The job itself
Policies and administration	Achievement
Supervision	Recognition for accomplishment
Working conditions	Challenging work
Interpersonal relations	Increased responsibility
Money, status, security	Growth and development

A significant finding for educational leaders is that the absence of dissatisfiers does not produce satisfaction on the job; however, the presence of dissatisfiers does bring about unhappiness in the worker. Only the presence of satisfiers, or motivators, brings about satisfaction in the worker.

Avoiding Job Dissatisfaction

A Formal, Systematic Orientation. When applying the theories of Herzberg to the concept of administrative support for the able teacher, the first matter which deserves attention is providing a positive work environment, thereby working to avoid dissatisfaction on the part of the teacher.

The first task in establishing the positive environment, following the selection of the instructor, is the orientation of the instructor. This orientation should be formalized, systematic, and preferably supplemented with handbooks, a series of handouts, or notebooks for the teacher. The following might be included in an orientation program for new teachers: a letter of welcome; a hiring packet; information on student attendance reporting; an organization chart; a school calendar; grade reporting information; policies and rules pertaining to printing, employee personal property, telephone usage, and purchasing supplies; bookstore operations information; information on the use of audiovisual equipment; and building and room access information. (The chapter by Carroll Londoner deals in greater detail with orientation and in-service education.)

Often a letter of agreement can also be used to provide the information needed by the instructor. The following is a sample letter of agreement.

Dear _____:

This memorandum of agreement between __(name of agency)__ and you serves to verify that you will teach __(name of course)__ on __(dates)__. You will be paid __(amount)__ for a minimum of __(number)__ registrants for the course. You will be paid an additional __(amount)__ for each enrollee beyond __(number)__ registrants. A maximum of __(number)__ will be allowed to register for the course.

You will receive payment on the first working day of the month following your last presentation.

Any seminar materials that you wish to have duplicated by this office should be submitted five (5) working days prior to the day of your presentation. Should you choose to have materials duplicated yourself, you may spend a maximum of $30.00. The invoice for printing must be submitted to this office for reimbursement.

Staff from this office will be available at the first class session to assist you. Please let me know if I can be of further assistance.

Please note, however, that if this course is canceled due to lack of enrollment, this contract shall be null and void.

After noting the conditions in this memorandum of agreement, please sign one copy and return it to this office to indicate acceptance.

Sincerely,

(Administrator)
_____

I have read the above memorandum of agreement and accept the terms therein.

_____
(Instructor)

Two copies of this letter should be sent along with a stamped, self-addressed envelope to ensure that a signed copy is returned for your file. Other information required by your agency for payment of any stipend, such as the instructor's social security number, should also be requested.

The above letter can be modified for individuals who are selected to make a presentation for a class, conference, or workshop; it should provide all the essential information needed by the instructor.

Providing Positive Working Conditions. After the teacher has begun the instructional assignment, a number of specific considerations can help provide positive support.

Appointments. First, post a schedule of the times available for the teacher to meet with the administrator. All too often the continuing education teacher works at night, while the administrator works during the day. The administrator is often out of the office at meetings or other activities, and the part-time teacher does not have easy access to him or her to discuss specific problems. The wise administrator will maintain office hours at a time when part-time teachers will be in the building.

When the teacher does meet with the administrator, attention should be focused on the teacher. This means that papers and other busy work will be put aside, and the teacher will be given the full attention of the administrator. All too often the teacher manages to see the administrator only on an unscheduled basis, and the administrator has a time conflict. Signing documents, for example, is an effective use of the administrator's time but is often taken as a lack of interest by the teacher. It is more effective to provide an appropriate time when full attention can be devoted to the teacher and his or her needs.

Budgetary Needs. It is essential to secure budgetary information from teachers on their needs for instructional materials and equipment. The teacher of adults is generally a part-time employee and not included in budget decisions. It is therefore important to provide a way for that teacher to provide input on his or her needs when building a budget for the program.

Support Services. Readily available secretarial and duplication services can greatly enhance the work environment for the part-time teacher. Having audiovisual equipment available during the hours when adult education classes regularly meet is an essential support service.

Physical Conditions. Will the available heat and light be suitable? Is the size of the assigned room appropriate for the anticipated enrollment? Is the furniture the correct size for adult students? Is access to the room easy? Is adequate parking available? Is smoking to be allowed? Where?

Timely Provision of Information. Class lists with the names of all students should be provided before the first class meeting, along with information on how drop-in students should be handled. A method for informing the teacher of canceled courses should be clarified.

Supervision and Interpersonal Relations. An important but difficult area in supervision is the need for honesty toward the teacher. Honesty and openness are required but often avoided when discussing the possible future of the course or the possibility of a permanent, tenure-type position or regular contract for the teacher. Often there is information that the teacher hopes not to hear, and consequently the administrator tends to avoid sharing it with the teacher. Moreover, when the teacher is working part-time, he or she is denied the "grapevine" channels of communication. When the hiring decisions become public and the course is canceled or filled by another teacher for the next term, the teacher will realize that information was withheld by the supervisor, and job dissatisfaction will result.

Money, Status, Security. Herzberg contends that money is also a potential job dissatisfier. Usually the continuing education teacher agrees to present a program or course for a set amount of money.

The issue of compensation for part-time teachers of adults is complex. The administrator is caught in the conflict between running a quality program—usually on a limited budget and therefore with fairly low and often fixed rates of pay—and providing differentiated rates of pay based on education and experience.

Pay Policies. There are a number of pay policies in use, including a flat hourly rate for all teachers; differential hourly rates based on qualifications, merit, or years of experience; the percentage of full-time teaching salaries; and incentive pay plans whereby teachers are paid on the basis of a percentage of fees paid, with either minimum or maximum enrollment limits as options. The administrator of continuing education must clearly understand the issues involved in establishing and operating under any pay policy selected by the institution. A policy of paying a flat rate for teaching a course, regardless of the teacher's background and experience, allows for easy budget planning and the selection of the best teacher interested in teaching the program without concern for fiscal impact. However, teachers may become dissatisfied when they feel that no recognition is given to their years of service, their qualifications, or the complexity of the subject offered.

Equality. An institution might be in danger of a lawsuit if it is found that the engineering instructors, who are all male, are routinely paid more than the sewing teachers, who are all female; and this must be taken into account.

The establishment of a pay policy for part-time teachers of adults is a potential minefield for the administrator. The budgeting needs of the program must be carefully balanced against the legitimate concerns of the part-time teachers. When making decisions about pay policy, the administrator should look carefully at ways to avoid job dissatisfaction because of salary. There must be equity among teachers for comparable work in relation to the rate paid. Once it is learned that there are unequal rates, and that personal "bargaining" for a salary is possible, the administrator will be forced to deal with some unhappy teachers. Instead, it is wise to have a clearly defined pay scale, in writing, with all factors explained to the teacher at the time of hiring.

Understanding Payroll Procedures. The administrator must make sure that any paperwork related to receiving the paycheck is understood completely and that deadlines for submission of any records or time sheets are made clear. The administrator may make a special effort to ensure that the time sheet is turned in properly for the first month of work, if that is the responsibility of the teacher. If the teacher is to be paid once only, the administrator should make every effort to see that that payment is made promptly. Finally, the administrator should make the teacher aware of the method of payment, including whether the check is to be mailed to the home or picked up and the dates on which checks are made available.

Herzberg's hygiene theory provides administrators with a framework for evaluating to what extent the work environments they provide lead to teacher satisfaction. The effective administrator must look beyond hygiene factors toward ways in which he or she can provide motivating conditions that will encourage teachers to give superior performances.

Motivating Teachers of Adults

Herzberg defines motivating factors as those which involve feelings of achievement, professional growth, recognition for accomplishment, and challenging work. These factors, which he calls the motivators, have a positive effect on job satisfaction and often produce an improvement in job performance.

Sergiovanni (1975) provides a useful overview of the application of Herzberg's theory to teacher supervision. He defines the motivation factors as those factors which are not automatically part of the job but which can generally be built into the job. These motivation factors encourage the teacher to go beyond the limits of the legal requirements of the job, such as preparing lessons, giving lectures, and grading students, and to give superior courses of study.

How then can the administrator provide these positive motivators to teachers of adults?

Special Efforts. The administrator should recognize the need for special efforts in this direction, especially when the teacher works on a part-time basis and is denied the regular peer support of the instructional community.

Involvement. The administrator should also design ways to involve continuing education teachers so that they will feel a part of the agency. This may be done by involvement of the teacher in developing courses or by working on the planning of special workshop sessions or summer offerings. The key, however, is the regular involvement of the teacher in a meaningful way in the decision making of the agency.

Informal Gatherings. To help the part-time teacher feel more involved, social activities or in-service activities that include a meal or extended coffee break should be offered. They should be scheduled at a time when all staff members, including the part-time teachers who often work in the evening, can attend. Some agencies have found that Friday afternoon meetings permit participation by all, as there are seldom courses scheduled for that evening.

Feeling of Territory. Administrators should recognize that part-time teachers, as well as full-time teachers, have this need. Ideally an office or desk should be assigned, but the teacher should at least be provided with a locking filing cabinet and a place where he or she can meet with students away from the classroom.

Access. Special arrangements need to be made to solve such problems as easy access to printing and to office communications. When the secretary's office closes and telephone messages cannot be received or access to reproduction facilities is unavailable, the teacher is unlikely to be motivated to work on preparing learning activites for the students.

Understanding. The teacher needs to feel that the course that he or she is teaching is really understood by the administrator. A good vehicle for this is the students' evaluations of the course. The evaluation process should be designed to formally communicate the results of student responses to the course content and to the manner of presentation. The data should be reviewed by the administrator, who can summarize and share the results with the teacher, either in writing or in a conference. The primary purpose of this process is to provide a vehicle for communication between the teacher and the administrator. The administrator can become involved in judging the quality of the course content and the satisfaction of students for whom the course is intended. The administrator should always keep in mind that an important outcome of evaluation is providing recognition for the teacher's accomplishment. In this way course evaluations can serve as a powerful motivator to the able teacher.

Public Recognition. This can be provided by means of a suitable title, such as "adjunct professor," which can be used by the teacher or in publicity using the mass media. This serves to provide important reinforcement for the job of teaching adults.

Professional Growth and Development. In-service experiences within the institution can be provided, or attendance at conferences or visits to other sites can be supported. The enrichment gained from allowing the teacher to expand his or her knowledge and to have the responsibility of representing the institution will be carried back to the classroom and to other colleagues.

Collective Bargaining as an Emerging Force

As interest in providing part-time educational opportunities for adults continues to expand, labor unions are becoming concerned with bargaining for part-time teachers. While administrators in business and industry have long been accustomed to participating in the collective bargaining process, administrators in education now have to work in new ways with labor unions in shared decision making.

Beverly Watkins (1979) cites a recent position paper issued by the American Federation of Teachers' advisory committee on higher education urging that local unions make strong drives to unionize part-time instructors. The statement ends with the argument that a cohesive faculty group, composed of both full- and part-time instructors, has the potential of a powerful pressure group with great political influence.

This and other developments have important implications for the topic of this chapter. Labor unions traditionally and constantly seek to change the work environment (Herzberg's dissatisfiers or hygiene factors). Some of the issues raised by the above committee include limiting the number of adjunct faculty members, dividing a full-time position into several part-time positions, and using part-time instructors as "strike breakers." Some of the goals suggested include the participation of part-time staff in academic activities; access to such professional perquisites as office space, secretarial help, and a mailbox; and the inclusion of both full- and part-time faculty members in a single bargaining unit.

However, the emergence of collective bargaining in continuing education will in no way reduce the need for administrative concern with job dissatisfiers and job motivators.

Summary

The administrator of able teachers of adults will improve his or her effectiveness in providing positive administrative support if a theory that provides a framework for administration is accepted and followed. Herzberg's motivation-hygiene theory provides such a framework. The able administrator will first look toward providing a conducive working environment for the teacher, because without a positive environment the teacher will be dissatisfied with the job assignment. But the administrator will also look beyond the job environment toward ways of providing positive motivation to the teacher, thereby helping to provide the best possible instruction to the adult student.

References

Argyris, C. *Personality and Organization.* New York: Harper & Row, 1957.
Herzberg, F., Mausner, B., and Snyderman, B. B. *The Motivation To Work.* New York: Wiley, 1959.
McGregor, D. *The Human Side of Enterprise.* New York: McGraw-Hill, 1960.
Maslow, A. H. *Motivation and Personality.* New York: Harper & Row, 1954.
Sergiovanni, T. J. (Ed.). *Professional Supervision for Professional Teachers.* Washington, D.C.: Association for Supervision and Curriculum Development, 1975.
Watkins, B. "AFT to Press for Unionization of Part-Timers." *Chronicle of Higher Education,* July 16, 1979, p. 1.

Delight C. Willing is dean of instruction and supervisor of adult education at Renton Vocational Technical Institute, Renton, Washington.

Continuing education administrators need to recognize and act on the full range of extrinsic and intrinsic rewards that motivate able teachers.

Developing a Comprehensive Reward System

James C. Votruba

The incentives that motivate teachers to become involved in continuing education are many and varied. For some, teaching adults may provide the opportunity for additional income. For others, it may provide the opportunity to stay current in their professional fields through interaction with practitioners. Some hope for new insights into their disciplines through working with older, more experienced students. Others simply enjoy the challenge and satisfaction of helping adult students develop and grow. If asked to describe their motivations, many teachers of adults would mention all these and more.

The challenge for the continuing education administrator is to develop and maintain a comprehensive reward system that appeals to able teachers of adults in as many ways as possible. The strategy for accomplishing this objective is a three-stage process. First, continuing education administrators should develop a perceptive insight into both the extrinsic and intrinsic rewards that are likely to motivate the teachers whom they hope to recruit and retain. Unfortunately, administrators far too often focus exclusively on the extrinsic incentives, such as money and fringe benefits, and overlook the equally important intrinsic incentives, such as recognition, self-esteem, and enjoyment. Second, based on a broad understanding of teacher motivation, a comprehensive reward system should be designed and implemented to appeal to as many of these motivations as possible. Third, a communication network should be established to effectively link the present and potential teachers of adults with the range of benefits that are available to them as a result of their involvement in continuing education. This chapter examines these three stages and suggests ways in which each can be accomplished.

Understanding Teacher Motivation

Continuing education administrators make a critical error when they fail to take into account the full range of motivations that prompt teachers to become involved in the instruction of adults. Maslow (1954) suggests that human beings are motivated by a broad range of human needs and concerns including security, affiliation, esteem, autonomy, and self-actualization. From the rather limited literature on the subject, it would appear that these basic motivations identified by Maslow are often influential in the decision of teachers to become involved in adult instruction.

Extrinsic Motivators. Most studies on why people teach adults have focused on full-time faculty members in collegiate settings who teach adults on a part-time basis. For example, much of the literature on motivation supports the assertion that decisions by faculty members to teach adults are influenced by the extent to which their institution will reward them for this type of instructional activity. Hanna (1978) suggests that these institutional rewards are usually and most powerfully realized through the salary, promotion, and tenure system, and that without adequate extrinsic rewards of this sort the recruitment and retention of faculty members to teach in continuing education is more difficult.

Patton (1975) concludes that incentives designed to attract individual faculty members and encourage departmental participation in extended degree programs need to emphasize financial perquisites as well as enhanced promotional opportunities. Knox (1975) and Strother (1974) also emphasize the importance of adequate institutional rewards in the effort to attract the most able faculty members to participate in the instruction of adults.

Votruba (1978) argues that faculty members devote most of their time and energy to the activities with the greatest potential for institutional and professional reward. Unless continuing education instruction is more fully integrated into the traditional faculty reward system as a criterion for salary, promotion, and tenure, continuing educators will find it difficult to attract and retain the ablest teachers of adults.

Intrinsic Motivators. While extrinsic rewards are undoubtedly powerful incentives for teaching adults, they are not the only sources of motivation. A substantial amount of evidence suggests that certain intrinsic rewards may provide as strong or stronger incentive.

Professional Opportunities. Medsker (1975) found that faculty members are motivated to participate in adult extended degree programs because of the opportunity for innovation, experimentation, and association with professionals in their field. These conclusions are further supported by Hanna (1978), who suggests that faculty members at a large midwestern university participated in continuing education activities more for intangible personal and professional reasons than for reasons related to financial or academic rewards or recognition.

Recognition. In a general study of faculty motivation, Tarvin (1972) found that faculty members rated nonmaterial rewards such as recognition as more important than material rewards. He adds, however, that failure to reward faculty performance in material terms such as salary, promotion, and tenure may negatively affect subsequent motivation.

Satisfaction. Bock (1976) found that the most important incentive for faculty involvement in teaching adults was the satisfaction they received and the good feelings that resulted from interaction with adult groups. Other strong motivators included community service, making friends for the university, identifying new topics of research, and enrichment of on-campus teaching as a result of continuing education involvement.

Votruba, Kozoll, and Anderson (1976) asked collegiate faculty members what motivated them to teach in continuing education programs. In order of frequency, the responses they received included staying in contact with their profession, staying current with the conditions in the field, making additional income, teaching more mature students, and helping to solve current problems.

Satisfiers and Dissatisfiers. Herzberg and others (1966) offered a particularly useful perspective when considering what motivates teachers to become involved in adult instruction. They suggested that the factors contributing to job satisfaction and the factors contributing to job dissatisfaction are actually two different sets. Factors from one set ("satisfiers") contribute to job satisfaction if present but not to job dissatisfaction when absent, while factors from the other set ("dissatisfiers") lead to dissatisfaction when not present but not to satisfaction when present. Herzberg goes on to suggest that satisfiers are directly related to intrinsic factors derived from the work itself. These include achievement, recognition, increased self-confidence, responsibility, and pleasure from the work itself. Dissatisfiers, however, are directly related to extrinsic factors associated with the work. These include salary, fringe benefits, working conditions, and the policies and procedures that govern the work environment. (See the chapter by Delight Willing for further discussion of Herzberg's theory.)

For the continuing educator, Herzberg's message suggests that what needs to be done is to maximize the intrinsic satisfiers related to teaching adults while minimizing the extent to which extrinsic factors cause dissatisfaction. More will be said later about how to accomplish this two-fold objective.

Negative Motivators. These may include "offers that cannot be refused" from deans or department heads, feelings of job insecurity because of a drop in institutional or departmental enrollment, and pressure from colleagues to be more productive in ways that result in tangible benefit for their academic units. Under such circumstances, it is doubtful that teachers are motivated to contribute more than the minimum amount of time and energy to adult instruction. Administrators should closely monitor the performance of these faculty members and try to translate what was initially a negative incentive for participation into more positive benefits and rewards.

Other Categories of Teachers. Most of the preceding discussion of intrinsic and extrinsic incentives has focused on full-time university faculty members who teach part-time in evening or off-campus courses for additional money. There are, of course, other categories of teachers whose motives for helping adults to learn can contribute to our understanding of how to develop more effective rewards for continuing education teachers.

Public school adult basic education (ABE) employs both full- and part-time teachers in day and evening programs. Understandably, their decision to accept or to remain in a full-time position is influenced by the rewards they receive. Incentives for those who teach full-time or part-time in ABE programs are suggested by studies of teacher competencies (Mocker, 1974; Zinn, 1974) and job status (Park, 1977), by evaluations of in-service workshops and staff development projects (Hansen, Klink, and Kramer, 1973; Kincaid and Rink, 1972), and by materials to orient new teachers (Ulmer, 1969). It is clear that assistance with understanding and relating to the clientele and with practical program development procedures is an important incentive for those who teach less advantaged adults.

In many segments of continuing education, those who teach adults do so as a secondary occupation. Such teachers are found in many occupational fields. They have become expert in the specialized topics they teach (Grabowski, 1976; Messerschmidt, 1967). Helping them become proficient teachers of adults can be a major incentive for their participation.

Techniques. Developing and maintaining a more precise understanding of what motivates teachers to become involved in adult instruction can be accomplished in several ways. Surveys of teachers currently involved in adult instruction can identify individual motivation. Surveys of potential teachers of adults can provide insight into what might motivate them to become involved. Current teachers of adults can be assembled in small groups to discuss the ways in which other teachers might be influenced to participate in continuing education programs. Questionnaires can be sent to instructors who have just finished teaching a continuing education program asking them to describe the various satisfiers and dissatisfiers associated with their participation. Administrators can conduct formal and informal interviews with teachers of adults to ascertain their motivation for participating.

Continuing educators need to pay close attention to all the extrinsic and intrinsic rewards that motivate teachers and prompt their involvement in continuing education programs. Once this sensitivity to teacher motivation is developed, continuing education administrators can begin to identify a range of rewards that will be responsive to as many of those motivations as possible.

Relating Rewards to Motivation

This review of incentives suggests that the motivation to become involved in adult instruction often involves a combination of perceived extrinsic rewards usually provided by the sponsoring agency and intrinsic rewards that derive from the work itself. I will now focus on the specific ways in which both types of rewards can be strengthened and expanded in one institutional setting—higher education.

Strengthening Extrinsic Rewards. The value that a collegiate institution places on various types of faculty professional activity can be assessed by observing how those activities are rewarded. Historically, colleges and universities have often had a difficult time recruiting faculty participation in continuing education activities because the primary faculty reward system provided little if any incentive for such involvement. Given a choice, most faculty members choose to devote the bulk of their time and energy to activities that are valued by their institution and rewarded at salary, promotion, and tenure time.

If our goal is to strengthen faculty motivation to participate in continuing education activities, we need first to look at the extent to which those activities are acknowledged as important by the institution and integrated into the primary faculty reward system. The process of achieving this integration is often difficult. Nevertheless, there are several steps that can be taken to facilitate the integrative process.

Faculty Reward Policies. A first step toward integration is to broaden and strengthen official campus policies related to rewards for faculty continuing education activity. For example, several years ago the faculty senate at the University of Illinois' Urbana campus unanimously passed the following resolution: "Campus- and college-level policies and procedures should be modified so that there are greater incentives and rewards for high-quality faculty participation as resource persons in university-sponsored continuing education and public service activities. The senate urges the chancellor to circulate this report and recommendations to the colleges and other administrative units with his recommendation for favorable consideration and implementation."

This kind of policy statement reinforces the legitimacy of continuing education activities while establishing a set of expectations for colleges and departments. Combined with a strong public commitment from the institution's chief academic officers, these policy statements can have a substantial influence on the willingness of department, college, and campus promotion and tenure committee members to reward creative and innovative faculty accomplishments in continuing education activities.

Developing a Process for Assessing Quality. This is needed to assess the quality of faculty continuing education efforts. The University of Illinois' Urbana campus provides a current example of this kind of effort. In 1976 the vice-chancellor for academic affairs constituted a faculty committee and charged it with developing guidelines for assessing the quality of faculty outreach efforts. The committee reported its recommendations in the spring of 1978. Soon thereafter a three-member project team was formed in the office of continuing education and public service to further define and implement the committee recommendations. With the support of the vice-chancellor for academic affairs, the project team sought out the involvement and assistance of campus promotion and tenure committee members, college and departmental chief executive officers, and selected faculty members. The result to date has been the development of an evaluative process for continuing education activity that has the acceptance and support of a broad cross-section of the academic community.

Working with Faculty Members. Continuing educators must work with faculty members to support and document the quality of their continuing education efforts. The development of qualitative indices serves little purpose if data are not collected, assembled, and brought to the attention of faculty colleagues and academic officers as evidence of achievement in outreach activities. Continuing education administrators can help faculty members design outreach activities that are consistent with the faculty reward system and then assist in the evaluation of those activities based on criteria acceptable to the campus community.

Relating Continuing Education to Campus Academic Goals. Colleges and departments will naturally encourage faculty participation in continuing education activities to the extent that they see these activities as consistent with their own goals and priorities. For example, many colleges of education are experiencing a substantial drop in on-campus enrollment. The same is true of many humanities departments. To the extent that continuing education administrators are sensitive to these concerns and can assist in the increase of off-campus enrollments, the academic unit will quite likely encourage faculty participation. Colleges and departments that encourage faculty participation in continuing education activities to satisfy their own priorities and goals incur an obligation to reward excellence in such activities.

Supporting Creative Efforts. Campus outreach offices might set aside a small fund each year that would be available on a competitive basis to support creative continuing education efforts. Given tangible financial and staff support, faculty members will be encouraged to develop innovative projects that serve the campus outreach mission as well as their own professional goals.

Traditionally, many collegiate institutions have given annual awards to faculty members for outstanding teaching and scholarship. These awards are highly visible and often include a monetary gift for both the faculty member and the department. The development of analogous awards for creativity in continuing education instruction would serve to underscore the importance of these activities. Campuses might establish awards for outstanding adult teaching, outstanding public service projects, and the most innovative outreach program. Such awards would provide highly visible recognition for faculty members and also reinforce the fact that creativity and excellence in continuing education and public service are worthwhile goals. The recognition of excellent programs and of outstanding faculty efforts by the National University Extension Association has served these purposes.

Campus outreach offices can also provide technical expertise and staff support to faculty members who are involved in outreach efforts. Assistance can be provided in identifying outside support for various types of continuing education. Help can be provided in developing and writing grant proposals. Journals can be identified in which faculty members might publish the significant results of their outreach efforts.

Providing Other Types of Institutional Rewards. Continuing education administrators can work to ensure that faculty overload pay, honoraria, and fringe benefits for outreach involvement are as competitive as possible. Faculty members who are recruited from outside the institution can be awarded an adjunct rank such as "adjunct professor" or "visiting professor" that acknowledges their affiliation with the institution. Faculty members who have completed continuing education activities can be sent letters thanking them for their participation and acknowledging their unique contributions. Copies of these letters can be sent to appropriate deans and department heads to officially acknowledge the faculty member's value to the program as well as the program's general significance.

Integrating Rewards into the Primary Reward System. This is often not an easy task and requires the strong support of the chief academic officers at the departmental, college, and campus levels. Nevertheless, if continuing education administrators are to recruit and retain the broad participation of campus faculty, this integration needs to be achieved.

Strengthening Intrinsic Rewards. As important as it is to develop extrinsic rewards for faculty outreach activity, it is clear from the literature that faculty members generally list intrinsic benefits as the primary reason for their continuing education activity. It is also in the area of intrinsic rewards, derived from the experience itself, that administrators may exercise their strongest and most creative initiative.

A faculty member's interest in planning and conducting continuing education activities is enhanced if he or she perceives a link between those activities and his or her own professional interests and objectives. Administrators of university outreach units can exercise considerable initiative in assisting the faculty members to recognize the professional benefits that result from conducting various continuing education activities.

Professional Benefits. Faculty members who have engaged in outreach activities often cite the following benefits as particularly important:

1. Interaction with professional practitioners helps them stay up to date in the fields related to their academic disciplines.

2. The problems raised by practitioners often stimulate them to explore the application of existing theory and knowledge to new and varied circumstances. This, in turn, can lead to new theory and knowledge.

3. Teaching older and more experienced students can lead to new interpretations and new ways of looking at traditional academic subject matter.

4. Part-time students and nontraditional teaching-learning settings often require the development of new instructional approaches that may also benefit full-time students in traditional settings.

5. Interaction with professional practitioners can lead to new research and scholarly activities.

6. Involvement in continuing education can lead to the enhancement of the professional prestige and visibility of the faculty member away from his or her own campus. This, in turn, may lead to more opportunities for consultation and public speaking.

These intrinsic benefits can make a substantial contribution to the self-respect, self-esteem, self-confidence, autonomy, and self-actualization of the individual faculty member. They can also bring the faculty member increased visibility, recognition, and respect from colleagues. In addition, intrinsic benefits may also lead to greater extrinsic institutional rewards. For example, the insights that result from the application of existing theory and knowledge to new circumstances may lead to journal publications that benefit the faculty member in the salary, promotion, and tenure process. Continuing educators need to underscore these benefits and match them with faculty motivations and priorities.

Status and Affiliation. In addition, faculty advisory groups can assist the continuing education administrator in setting policies and procedures that govern campus outreach activities. Involvement in these groups can provide faculty members with a sense of control over their work environment, a sense of status in their policy-making role, and a sense of affiliation and community as they work as a group on common issues and concerns.

Developing a spirit of association and community is very important. While there may be hundreds of faculty members on campus who are involved in continuing education activities, they are often only a small minority in their particular college, school, or department. This sense of isolation can be offset if continuing educators develop ways for faculty members from various disciplines to interact with each other on a recurring basis. This may be achieved through faculty advisory groups, planning committees, new faculty orientation, periodic seminars that outreach faculty are invited to attend and participate in, and annual programs to honor faculty for long or distinguished service to the campus outreach mission. The objective in this regard is to develop a sense of community among the faculty members who are engaged in continuing education activities. This sense of association around commonly shared commitments, experiences, and understanding can provide strong support and incentive for faculty to remain involved.

Minimizing Dissatisfiers. Most of the discussion up to now has focused on job satisfiers. However, while strengthening and expanding the extrinsic and intrinsic motivations for faculty outreach participation, administrators also need to ensure that the conditions of outreach involvement are not having a negative impact on participation.

Assume that a university faculty member has recently agreed to teach an off-campus credit course in a location approximately one hundred miles away. When he receives his assignment he is not told where the class is being held, when it will begin, how to schedule a university car, or the procedure for travel advances and expense reimbursement. He is also not sure how to order textbooks, when and where they will be delivered, and in what manner payment should be made. On top of all this, he is being paid far less than what he would expect on the basis of his on-campus salary.

The first night of class he arrives at the building and finds all doors locked. He finally finds a night custodian who mumbles something about not being informed but unlocks the classroom. The students arrive and begin asking questions regarding off-campus enrollment procedures. The instructor does not have the information. The outside temperature is 90 degrees, and the room is not air-conditioned. Finally the class is over and the instructor prepares to go have dinner before driving home. He has no idea where to find a good restaurant, gets lost in the process of his search, and finally arives home at midnight. The next morning he says to his wife, "I enjoy working with adults but I don't know if it's worth the hassle."

With early and complete information, proper orientation, and greater attention to class scheduling, this experience could have been made far more enjoyable for the faculty member involved. These dissatisfiers can severely undermine the positive benefits that a faculty member can and should experience as part of his or her outreach involvement. Continuing education administrators need to take every initiative to see that dissatisfiers are kept under control.

Communicating Rewards

The development of a comprehensive system of faculty rewards for outreach involvement serves little purpose if it is not effectively communicated in a way that promotes a positive faculty response. Continuing educators can exercise considerable initiative in facilitating this communication process.

The strength of a message is often influenced by the messenger. In this regard, continuing educators need to enlist the assistance of faculty members to educate their own colleagues regarding the benefits that accrue from continuing education and public service involvement. Communication regarding these benefits achieves greater strength and legitimacy if it comes from a colleague whom the faculty member knows, trusts, and respects.

This communication through "significant others" can occur in a variety of ways. Continuing educators may choose to publish outreach newsletters in which faculty members describe recent outreach activities. Appropriate topics may include the application of existing theory and knowledge to new and varied contexts, the development of new disciplinary insights as a result of interaction with adult students, and the creation of new curricular designs, instructional delivery approaches, or teaching methods, designed to meet the particular needs of adult students. Also included in such newsletters should be announcements of faculty awards for outreach involvement, a list of publications resulting from outreach activity, and funding opportunities for outreach teaching and research.

At a less formal level, administrators who hope to encourage increased involvement by the faculty of a particular college or department may choose to enlist faculty members from units that already have substantial outreach experience. These experienced faculty members can help familiarize their colleagues with the various benefits of involvement. The value of this approach is of course strengthened to the extent that the experienced faculty member is an opinion leader in the academic unit and enjoys the respect and trust of his or her colleagues.

Administrators enhance the likelihood of effective communication of rewards if they routinely ask themselves two important questions. First, to whom do I want to communicate these rewards and benefits? The answer may be a single faculty member or the faculty members of a department, college, or entire campus. Second, who are the "significant others" who influence these faculty members' attitudes and behaviors? Once these questions are answered, administrators can begin developing the message and recruiting the messengers.

If the college or university is to provide a strong supportive environment for faculty involvement in continuing education, then institutional policy makers need to be kept informed of the institutional benefits that accrue from outreach activity. For example, continuing education programs offered in the evening frequently help strengthen relationships with business and industry, state and local government, alumni, and the local community. Programs that involve state and local problem solving can lead to increased credibility with the general public and stronger support from the legislature, governor, and state board of higher education. Continuing education administrators can take the initiative to keep institutional policy makers well informed regarding these institutional benefits.

Summary

Many incentives motivate teachers to become involved in continuing education, including, for some, the promise of extrinsic rewards provided by the sponsoring agency or institution. For others, the incentive may be the intrinsic rewards that derive from the teaching experience itself. In fact, the literature suggests that most teachers of adults are motivated by a combination of both extrinsic and intrinsic factors. The challenge to continuing educators is to develop a comprehensive system of rewards that appeals to as many of these motivations as possible. To the extent that teachers perceive their involvement in adult instruction as a way to gain in security, status, self-esteem, recognition, self-confidence, autonomy, influence, or self-actualization, they are more likely to become involved and remain involved in continuing education programs. Administrators make a critical error when they do not recognize and act upon the full range of incentives that prompt teachers to become involved in adult instruction.

A comprehensive reward system for teachers of adults can best be accomplished if administrators focus on three developmental stages. First, they should strive to develop a keen insight into both the extrinsic and intrinsic rewards that are likely to motivate teachers whom they hope to recruit and retain. Second, based on this broad understanding of teacher motivation, a comprehensive system of rewards should be designed to appeal to as many of these motivations as possible. Third, a communication network should be established to link present and potential teachers of adults with the full range of benefits that are available through their participation in continuing education programs. Focusing primarily on the higher education context, this chapter has suggested ways in which each of these stages can be effectively accomplished.

References

Bock, L. "Teaching Adults." *Humanities Forum*, March 1976. (Published by University of Illinois at Urbana-Champaign School of Humanities.)
Grabowski, S. M. *Training Teachers of Adults: Models and Summative Programs.* Syracuse, N.Y.: Syracuse University Press, 1976.
Hanna, E. "Faculty Participation in Continuing Education: A Case Study." Unpublished doctoral dissertation, Michigan State University, 1978.
Hansen, G. L., Klink, A. L., and Kramer, R. E. *Assessment and Programming for Personnel Development in Adult Education—State of Iowa.* Cedar Falls, Iowa: University of Northern Iowa, 1973.
Herzberg, F., and others. *Work and the Nature of Man.* New York: World, 1966.
Kinkaid, H. V., and Rink, D. L. *Preliminary Three Year Plan for Adult Basic Education Staff Development.* Menlo Park, Calif.: Stanford Research Institute, 1972.
Knox, A. B. "New Realities, the Administration of Continuing Higher Education." *NUEA Spectator*, December 1975, pp. 6-9.
Maslow, A. *Motivation and Personality.* New York: Harper & Row, 1954.
Medsker, L., and others. *Extending Opportunities for a College Degree: Practices, Problems, and Potentials.* Berkeley, Calif.: University of California Press, 1975, p. 175.
Messerschmidt, D. H. "A Study of Part-Time Instructors in Vocational-Technical Education Among Community Colleges in Michigan." Unpublished doctoral dissertation, Michigan State University, 1967.
Mocker, D. W. *A Report on the Identification, Classification, and Ranking of Competencies Appropriate for Adult Basic Education Teachers.* Kansas City: Center for Resource Development in Adult Education, University of Missouri-Kansas City, 1974.
Park, R. "Women in Adult Basic Education." *Lifelong Learning: The Adult Years*, 1977, *1* (4), 12-14.
Patton, C. V. "Extended Education in an Elite Institution: Are There Enough Incentives to Encourage Faculty Participation?" *Journal of Higher Education*, July 1975, *66* (4), 427-444.
Strother, G. B. "The University's Role in Public Service and Extension." In *Proceedings of National Conference on Public Service and Extension in Institutions of Higher Education.* Athens: University of Georgia, 1974, pp. 11-18.
Tarvin, L. "Faculty Motivation." Unpublished doctoral dissertation, Indiana University, 1972.
Ulmer, C. *Teaching the Disadvantaged Adult.* Washington, D.C.: National Association for Public School Adult Education, 1969.
Votruba, J. C. "Faculty Rewards for University Outreach: An Integrative Approach." *Journal of Higher Education*, 1978, *49* (1), 639-648.
Votruba, J. C., Kozoll, C. E., and Anderson, T. "A Profile of Extramural Faculty at the University of Illinois at Urbana-Champaign." Internal Report of the Office of Continuing Education and Public Service, University of Illinois, 1976, p. 1.
Zinn, L. M. *Adult Basic Education Teacher Competency Inventory: Iowa Final Report.* Kansas City: University of Missouri-Kansas City, Center for Resource Development in Adult Education, 1974.

James C. Votruba is associate director of the office of continuing education and public service and assistant professor of continuing and higher education at the University of Illinois at Urbana-Champaign.

Evaluation is like the weather; everybody talks about it, but few do anything about it.

Learning as a Criterion of Success

Donald W. Mocker

In continuing education, evaluation is an issue that is widely discussed and rarely acted upon. At the national level there has yet to be a study conducted that systematically looks at how well continuing education is working. While there has been more activity in evaluation at the state level, the quality of that activity cannot stand even mild scrutiny. At the local level, continuing education administrators are often too busy to do a complete evaluation of the teaching staff. They are often forced to make judgments about the quality of teaching based on student ratings of teachers or on certain observational techniques. These types of evaluation are often nothing more than crude scales (sometimes even just "happiness indexes"), which result in, at best, highly subjective judgments.

Although student ratings and observation techniques are often highly subjective, they can provide part—but only part—of the data an administrator needs to make judgments about the quality of teaching. In this chapter I will argue that student learning is often overlooked as a useful means of evaluation. An evaluation design that provides alternatives for using student ratings, administrator observation, and student learning will be presented. My assumption is that the evaluation of student learning is an essential component for evaluating teacher effectiveness. Otherwise the evaluation is incomplete, and the administrator runs the risk of making incorrect judgments.

What Is Evaluation?

At the beginning of the formal evaluation movement, evaluation was defined as a process for determining the extent to which the educational objectives were actually being achieved by the curriculum and instructional activities (Tyler, 1950). This definition was first proposed by Tyler as part of the eight year study during the late 1930s and early 1940s. Judgment has been an implicit part of evaluation, according to Scriven (1967) and Stake (1967). Today we broadly define evaluation as the collection of data on which judgments about the worth or value of something are made.

Scriven also identified two basic roles evaluation could play. The first is an on-going process with recurring feedback into the system. The purpose of this type of evaluation is to improve the program, and it is called "formative evaluation." The second concerns decisions about the value of the finished product. Traditionally in an instructional program this involves comparing the actual learning outcomes with the intended learning outcomes. Scriven calls this type "summative." The two types of evaluation are distinguished by the time during the program life at which the evaluation occurs and by the uses to which the data are put.

In any approach to evaluating teachers, it should be recognized that the value of the judgments made about teacher effectiveness stand in direct relation to the quality of the data collected. As evaluation procedures provide more thorough and objective data, the quality of the judgments will be improved.

Use of Evaluation in Continuing Education

Continuing education administrators must make many decisions as part of their jobs, including the following. How can evaluation be used to improve courses? What materials, methods, and instructional techniques need improvement? How can diagnosis be improved? (These deal with formative evaluation.) How good are the teachers? How good is the total program? (These deal with summative evaluation.)

The important question is not whether or not administrators make the above decisions. They all do. Some may do it formally and systematically report their results, while others do it informally and keep it to themselves. But decisions are made throughout each year by every administrator. The critical question then becomes on what basis, using what data and criteria, will the administrator make those decisions.

Strategies for Teacher Evaluation

The strategies proposed here include student rating of teachers, administrator rating of teachers, and the measurement of learning. The first two techniques are familiar to most administrators and will be only briefly reviewed. The third technique—using learning as a criterion of teacher success—will be discussed in greater depth. Other approaches to teacher evaluation could include peer evaluation and self-evaluation techniques by either the student or the teacher. However, these will not be discussed here.

Student Rating of Teachers. Student rating of teachers is a popular method of evaluation that seems to be gaining in use. Despite the difficulty of establishing their reliability, student ratings produce data from one important source, and if used as part of a total system, they can be a valuable tool. Doyle (1975) has analyzed various approaches to teacher evaluation and described how a system for the student rating of teachers could be implemented.

The most common format is a questionnaire in which the student is asked to rate the teacher according to a preestablished set of variables. Open-ended questions may also be included in which students are requested to make comments and suggestions.

Many studies have been conducted to establish the important variables that students will rate (Eble, 1970; Hildebrand and Wilson, 1970). These studies have identified the following teacher behaviors: clarity of organization, interpretation, and explanation; encouragement of class discussion and the presentation of various points of view; observable indications of interest in students; and demonstration of enthusiasm.

In addition to the problem of reliability, the major weakness of this technique is its use as the only evaluation tool. Studies by Gage (1961) have found that freshmen and sophomore classes give lower ratings than upper division classes. He also found that class size affected ratings and that lower-ranked professors were also consistently lower. Finally, Gage found that teachers who instructed elective courses were consistently rated higher.

Student ratings can provide helpful data to an administrator, but they are best used as part of a total teacher evaluation process.

Administrator Rating of Teachers. Another popular technique for evaluating teachers has been administrator observation and rating of teacher performance against a checklist of the traits of the ideal teacher.

Trying to decide what makes a "competent" teacher is a problem that has occupied the attention of researchers and practitioners for many years. The birth of the accountability movement in the 1950s and the student protests of the 1960s have given new life to the search. In adult education many studies have been conducted to develop competency lists of the model teacher (Bruny, 1970; Fenn, 1972; Knowles, 1970; Mocker, 1974; Niemi and Davison, 1971; Smith, 1972).

Burkhart (1969) reviewed 1,000 studies on the subject of what is a good teacher. The vast majority of studies used some form of rating scale to make subjective judgments about teacher success.

The major problem with observational techniques is the ephemeral nature of the classroom. The quantity and quality of learning is not something that is always observable. What is observable in any class on any given day is unique to a teacher's personality, the learners, and the instructional intent of the teacher. There has been little agreement on the criteria that describe an effective teacher.

Learning As Criterion of Teacher Success. Tyler (1950) suggested an evaluation model for appraising the changes of behavior (especially the learning) of students. In practice, however, little attention has been given to student learning as the criterion for measuring either teacher or program success. In the Burkhart (1969) study reported above, only 20 of 1,000 studies had used student learning as a criterion of success.

Recently, much interest has focused on student mastery of prespecified instructional objectives as a major criterion for measuring teacher effectiveness. Behavioral objectives have been used to define what was being evaluated. Teachers were asked to direct their teaching toward specific instructional objectives, and they were judged on the amount of pupil growth in those areas. The problem with these studies has been the lack of valid and reliable instruments that can be easily and efficiently developed and used by administrators and teachers.

In a study of student teachers, Moffett (1967) showed that teachers received more satisfaction from teaching an experimental group of students who achieved their instructional goals than from teaching a control group who did not. McNeil (1966) used a similar method in which the supervisor and teacher agree in advance on what will be used to judge the change in student behavior. It appears that student gains are greater when the teacher expects to be evaluated on the basis of those gains.

Problems in Using Learning as a Criterion. When learning is used as the criterion for judging teacher effectiveness, there are problems that must be solved if the administrator is to make objective judgments. First, there is the problem of time. If end-of-the-course achievement is used to judge student learning, many events happen during that time that are beyond the control of the teacher. These variables have a powerful effect on learning and must be considered when evaluating how much was learned. Some students may change their personal goals; others may have family problems that take priority; and still others may move or change jobs and can no longer attend class. These events happen in continuing education programs, and all affect learning. Any evaluation model that uses learning as the criterion for judging effectiveness must take these influences into consideration.

Second, there is the problem of whether or not the learner has an adequate background for the content of the course (sometimes referred to as a prerequisite).

Third, the evaluation technique must be practical. Administrators often have teachers who are located at various sites. Usually there is only a small staff to supervise these teachers. For an evaluation technique to be practical, it must produce adequate and valid data in whatever amount of time an administrator has.

Targeted Evaluation Approach

Although there is a role for student rating and administrator observation, I believe that without student learning as a measure of teacher success evaluation is incomplete. Although adult learning occurs in many settings—on the job, in a course at home, during leisure activities—most teachers of adults are involved in group instruction. I have adapted the logical instruction model developed by Pierce and Lorber (1977) as a means for collecting data about teacher effectiveness. This target evaluation approach (TEA) is designed to measure how much adults learn, while at the same time controlling for variables that are beyond the control of the continuing education teacher.

The model was developed with the following criteria in mind: teachers must not be held accountable for variables affecting learning that are beyond their control, an evaluation model that is useful in continuing education must be simple to use and at the same time produce adequate and valid data, and the model must be flexible enough to be appropriate in a variety of settings with varied curriculums.

Figure 1. Example of Evaluation Model

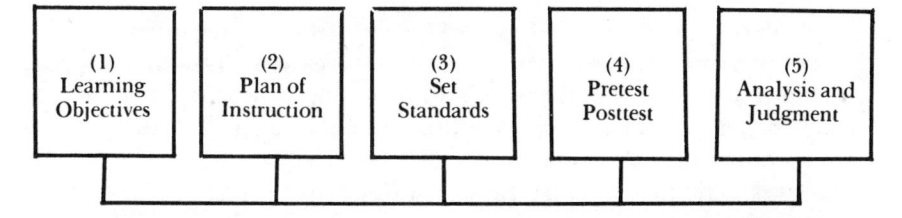

(1) Learning Objectives	(2) Plan of Instruction	(3) Set Standards	(4) Pretest Posttest	(5) Analysis and Judgment

The model does not introduce new technology but uses concepts and techniques that are already known. It was designed to be used in a single class period. Because of the variety of settings in continuing education, it would be inappropriate to specify an exact schedule. But some general hints can be given. If an adult basic education program involves class meetings two evenings a week, then the model can be used two or maybe three times a year. If the teachers are working full time with adults, then four or five times a year might be more appropriate. Regardless of the setting, it would not be wise to base an evaluation on a single instructional effort.

The model has five steps: writing objectives, developing a lesson plan, setting standards, constructing preassessment and postassessment instruments, and analyzing and judging the results.

Step 1: Writing Objectives. The teacher first identifies the portion of the content that can be taught in one class period. The content should not carry over to the next class, and content that requires little specific prior knowledge should be selected if possible. This will help avoid the problem of pretesting for any prerequisites.

The teacher then identifies the specific prerequisite background. For example, if the teacher is a vocational instructor teaching a general introductory course on electrical motors, careful attention to prior understanding would be necessary. Here, knowledge of simple circuitry, the laws of magnetism, and an understanding of the conversion of electromagnetic energy into mechanical energy is necessary. However, if the teacher is a macrame instructor in a general education program, it might be realistic to assume that no specific prior knowledge was necessary. It is true that a learner would need minimal manual dexterity, but it can be safely assumed that most adults enrolling for macrame would possess this.

As a rule of thumb, for a two-hour class session for adult basic education students, the teacher should have two (certainly no more than three) objectives. These objectives, in my judgment, should be written in behavioral terms using the criteria established by Mager (1962) or any other systematic approach. Continuing educators who have some formal preparation in education will have no difficulty in writing this type of objective. Teachers without this background can work individually through Mager's book and develop enough proficiency to enable them to write their own objectives.

Step 2: Developing a Lesson Plan. All teachers, regardless of their level of preparation in education, have some idea about how to teach, and the many techniques and procedures available to teachers will not be outlined here. What is important for the administrator is to have the teacher outline the lesson plan in detail. The teacher needs to identify the objectives, activities, resources, and techniques to be used for that particular lesson. If the lesson has been developed in detail and is in writing, then the administrator and the teacher can jointly evaluate it at the beginning (formulative evaluation) and at the end (summative evaluation).

Step 3: Setting Standards. The administrator and teacher must then agree on the standard of acceptable performance. For example, they might agree that 70 percent of the students should answer 80 percent of the questions correctly.

This decision will vary with the content and use to be made of the knowledge. For instance, in the macrame class the above standard might be acceptable, but in the mathematics class, where understanding of the foundations is essential, greater mastery may need to be achieved. Here, the teacher and administrator might agree that 90 percent of the students should answer 95 percent of the questions correctly. It is also probable that in some situations all the learners will need to score 100 percent on the test.

What this means to administrators is that there will not be a single standard for all teachers. There can be many standards, and the administrator and teacher need to determine a particular standard for the teacher's content area.

Step 4: Constructing Preassessment and Postassessment Instruments. Judgments on learning should only be made in the case of learners who have met the prerequisites and who have not previously learned the content. Preassessment is essential.

Once the prerequisites have been identified as part of determining objectives, two or three questions need to be written to test proficiency. Overtesting should be avoided, but care needs to be taken to assure that each prerequisite has been mastered by the learner.

The next task is to write four or five questions for the preassessment instrument that will adequately test the learner's knowledge of the content to be presented. Now the prerequisite questions and the content questions can be put together to make up the preassessment instrument. The preassessment content questions may also be used in the postassessment instrument. If not, alternative questions testing the same content need to be developed for the postassessment instrument.

Now all the elements are in place. The teacher has developed a single lesson with specific objectives and pre- and posttesting instruments. The teacher and administrator have agreed on the minimal standard for which the preassessment test is to be given at the first of the lesson. The lesson plan is then implemented; finally, at the completion of the lesson, the posttest is administered.

Step 5: Analyzing and Judging the Results. After the lesson is completed, the teacher scores the pretest and eliminates all those who did not meet the prerequisites and those who already knew the content. For those remaining, the posttest will be scored and gains computed. The administrator is now ready to make some judgment, based on this sample of a person's teaching. He or she may want to obtain additional data from other class periods.

Limitations of the TEA Approach. As with all evaluation techniques, the TEA approach has both strengths and weaknesses. It has three important limitations of which an administrator should be aware.

Because this approach is based on behavioral or measurable objectives, all the problems inherent in that system are brought to this technique. Eisner (1967) has identified some shortcomings of behavioral objectives. First, they are based on the assumption that the outcome of instruction can be predicted. He feels instruction is much too complex for this determination to be made in advance. Second, objectives do not account for the constraints some subjects—such as philosophy—place on objectives or for certain achievements that cannot be directly measured. Finally, Eisner has pointed out that the logic of objectives may not be flexible enough to account for the various conditions under which people learn.

Another limitation of this system is that it does not have norms. This may cause problems if the administrator is required to rank all teachers and only has data from this source to use as the criterion. Also, unintended learning outcomes are not recognized, although most administrators and teachers know that often the unintended outcomes in continuing education are as important as the intended outcomes.

Using the Data to Make Judgments

How Effective Is a Teacher? By looking at student ratings and administrative observation data and by comparing the actual learning with a standard of acceptable performance, an administrator can decide how effective a particular teacher has been. A successful teacher will be one whose students achieve the specific expectations that the teacher and administrator have set for that course. (As noted previously, different standards may be established for different teachers.)

Are There Instructional Weaknesses? If the preset standards are not met, then the teacher and administrator can begin an analysis to identify the possible shortcomings. Adjustments can be made in the objectives, the lesson plan, the pre- and posttests, and the standards themselves.

How Successful Is the Program? The administrator can combine data from all teachers and by computing averages can make general judgments about program success. For example, an administrator can report that 75 percent of the students responded correctly on 80 percent of the test items, rather than reporting that 75 percent of the students said they liked the teacher.

Summary

With the present level of development, no evaluation approach is foolproof. Each approach has its weaknesses and strengths. By using an approach that provides data from several sources, administrators become better equipped to make objective judgments about their programs and their faculties. The prudent administrator will carefully assess each evaluation strategy in terms of the purpose of the evaluation, acceptance by the teachers, appropriateness for the content area, and cost.

References

Bruny, S. P. "Educational and Experimental Backgrounds of Adult Educators in Franklin County, Ohio and Their Training Needs." Unpublished doctoral dissertation, Ohio State University, 1970.

Burkhart, R. C. (Ed.). "The Assessment Revolution: New Viewpoints for Teacher Education." Albany, N.Y.: New York State Education Department, 1969.
Doyle, K. D., Jr. *Student Evaluation of Instruction.* Lexington, Mass.: Heath, 1975.
Eble, K. E. *The Recognition and Evaluation of Teaching.* Salt Lake City, Utah: The Project to Improve College Teaching, 1970.
Eisner, E. W. "Educational Objectives: Help or Hindrance?" *School Review,* 1967, *75* (3), 250-260.
Fenn, N. E., Jr. "The Identification of Competencies Pertinent to the Certification of Teachers in Adult Basic Education." Unpublished doctoral dissertation, Florida State University, 1972.
Gage, N. L. "The Appraisal of College Teaching: Analysis of Ends and Means." *Journal of Higher Education,* 1961, *32* (1), 17-22.
Hildebrand, M., and Wilson, R. C. *Effective University Teaching and Its Evaluation.* Berkeley, Calif.: University of California, Center for Research and Development in Higher Education, 1970.
Knowles, M. *The Modern Practice of Adult Education.* New York: Association Press, 1970.
Mager, R. F. *Preparing Instructional Objectives.* Palo Alto, Calif.: Fearon, 1962.
McNeil, J. D. "Antidote to a School Scandal." *Educational Forum,* 1966, *31* (1), 69-77.
Mocker, D. M. "The Identification, Classification, and Ranking of Knowledge, Behaviors, and Attitudes Appropriate for Adult Basic Education Teachers." Unpublished doctoral dissertation, State University of New York, Albany, 1974.
Moffett, G. W. "Use of Instructional Objectives in the Supervision of Student Teachers." Unpublished doctoral dissertation, University of California, Los Angeles, 1967.
Niemi, J. A., and Davison, C. V. "The Adult Basic Education Teacher: A Model for Analysis for Training." *Continuous Learning,* 1971, *4* (10), 109-114.
Pierce, W. D., and Lorber, M. A. *Objectives and Methods for Secondary Teaching.* Englewood Cliffs, N.J.: Prentice-Hall, 1977.
Scriven, M. "The Methodology of Evaluation." In R. W. Tyler (Ed.), *Perspectives of Curriculum Evaluation.* Chicago: University of Chicago Press, 1967.
Smith, R. L. "A Study to Determine the Perceptions of the Competencies Needed by Adult Basic Education Teachers." Unpublished doctoral dissertation, Oregon State University, 1972.
Stake, R. E. "The Countenance of Educational Evaluation." *Teachers College Record,* 1967, *68* (7), 523-540.
Tyler, R. W. *Basic Principles of Curriculum and Instruction.* Chicago: University of Chicago Press, 1950.

Donald Mocker is professor of education in secondary and adult education at the School of Education, University of Missouri, Kansas City.

Continuing education administrators should be committed to examining their staffing practices and to making fundamental changes that contribute to effective learning experiences for adults.

New Directions for Attracting Able Teachers of Adults

Jerry Parsons

One of the hallmarks of adult and continuing education this decade has been the movement of the education of adults from the periphery to the center of the educational scene. Although the antecedents of this change are deeply rooted in the basic fabric of American society, it was not until this decade that the education of adults achieved some degree of acceptance by most educators. As individuals and as a society we have always known that lifelong learning was essential to our own development and to the effective implementation of the democratic principles of our government. The unique needs and concerns of individuals, organizations, and society as a whole in the 1970s created the climate for continuing education to be fully recognized as an integral part of the education establishment.

K. Patricia Cross (1979, p. 75) states that "adult learners constitute the most rapidly growing segment of American education." From 1969 to 1975 the number of adults in organized learning activities increased 30.8 percent, more than double their increase in the population (Cross, 1979). The number of adults participating in educational endeavors has catapulted the adult learner into prominence in educational institutions.

At the same time, educational institutions facing a decline in the number of traditional postsecondary school students have found that adult students—both full-time and part-time—can help fill their classrooms. One can argue against the merits of this reasoning, but the undeniable situation increases the respectability of continuing education.

Another contributing factor to the added stature of continuing education has been the rapidity of technological advances and the subsequent economic and social factors that have created tension in our society. One way to resolve this tension and to help adults cope with the change has been through continuing education.

Challenges and Choices

Educational practice tends to be slow in meeting the expectations of a new clientele. Where there has been a pressing need for added educational opportunities for adults, selected institutions have responded with additional continuing education opportunities. Now—as this challenge is being met—is the time to consolidate experiences and research on the implications for educational practice.

The authors of the preceding chapters have provided a framework for this to happen. Using their experiences and those of their colleagues, along with educational theory and research, they have synthesized a set of desirable educational practices. They have also, directly or indirectly, focused on issues, questions, and new directions for the selection and development of teachers of adults.

Barriers to Improvement. Perhaps the most striking observation from reviewing the preceding chapters is the embarrassing gap between what is espoused and what is actual practice. Our rhetoric far exceeds our performance; it would be difficult to find Buskey's plan for recruitment, Londoner's scheme for staff development, and Mocker's evaluation design in operation at the present time.

The field of continuing education is probably not alone in not practicing what is preached. But an examination of the barriers to improving staffing practices in continuing education is in order. What prevents the implementation of improvements in recruitment, for example? Do we need to give more time to think critically about what is a desirable approach in staff development? Is there a feeling that if we cannot do everything then we do nothing to evaluate teaching? Is more criticism implied when something is incomplete than when it is not even begun?

In response to the question of what continuing education administrators should attend to during the next decade, Buskey's call for a staff recruitment plan would be one suggestion. Conti and Porter's method of using tests as a screening device would be another. Each suggested practice should be field-tested and evaluated by continuing education administrators so that their conclusions could be shared.

Equal Opportunity. Affirmative action and equal opportunity regulations involve other questions for staff recruitment and selection policy and practice. This appears to be a changing area of administrative activity. Conti and Porter advise continuing education administrators to become fully informed of the legal requirements involved.

What more can administrators do to promote equal opportunity in the employment of teachers? Buskey recommends the use of advertisements as one source of identifying teachers; this could be particularly useful for encouraging applications from minority persons.

Search Committees. Conti and Porter also note the use of the search committee in the selection process. The growth in the use of this technique will probably continue as a way of fulfilling the expectations of the affirmative action legislation. While a search committee may be widely used for selecting full-time teachers, administrators should also consider its applicability to selecting part-time teachers. Some of the advantages of a search committee should be noted: it tends to enlarge the pool of applicants; it tends to prevent continually hiring one type of person; it tends to open up the process to others besides persons with inside information; and it usually results in employing able people. These advantages need to be weighed against the problems of cost (primarily in terms of the time involved) and the amount of time required to reach a decision.

Reliance on Part-Time Teachers. Although not specifically discussed in the previous chapters, this is an important issue. Obviously, many teaching assignments (such as a conference presentation or a one-time course offering) could never be developed into full-time teaching positions. But others, such as teaching academic subjects like basic education, high school or GED courses, and college or university courses could become full-time. Both administration and program development have evolved into full-time positions, and one could ask why there are not more opportunities for full-time teaching in adult education. It seems reasonable to assume that the development of a cadre of full-time teachers of adults would overcome some of the problems in staff development cited by Londoner. Even in rural areas, agencies could experiment with employing a full-time teacher to serve two or more schools or agencies.

Evaluation. The discussion of supervision and teacher evaluation raises several interrelated issues. Instituting any of the recommended procedures in this area necessarily involves the administrator in some delicate relationships with faculty members. There is a challenge here for the administrator to find appropriate roles and relationships. Obviously the authoritarian, supervisor-subordinate relationship is not workable. A collegial peer-relationship seems more appropriate, and that may take some careful working out of new perceptions and relationships by both administrator and teacher.

In some preparatory education settings, the classroom is the teacher's castle, and woe betide the administrator who intrudes upon it. If continuing education administrators are to establish the kind of helping relationship proposed by Brumfield and Nesbit, they will have to break down these taboos and establish an open and trusting relationship that permits counsel and assistance.

In working with teachers of adults, administrators cannot escape the fact that they can and do make judgments about teachers, which can interfere with the helping and counseling function. At this point the administrator should consider using faculty self-evaluation methods as a nonthreatening means of assessing teacher performance. The administrator can encourage faculty members to seek help in areas where it is needed and to suggest areas for emphasis in the staff development program for faculty members. Another useful approach is identifying a neutral party, such as an ombudsman, to give teachers assistance on a confidential basis. Many teachers would benefit from a support group experience in which they could interact with other teachers who have similar problems, concerns, and needs.

Changing Attitudes and Strategies. The chapters on administrative support and incentives describe a promising range of strategies. One wonders what are the barriers that prevent the widespread use of these excellent ideas. Some barriers—such as underfunding and limited staff—are certainly formidable. However, continuing education has surely progressed beyond the place where inadequate funds and inadequate time can explain away all deficiencies. Does the administrator run the program (or does the program run the administrator) from one harried sequence of deadlines to another? Has not the time arrived when administrators need to lay out the functions that are essential for the long-range good of the program and proceed from that point to staff and budget the program adequately? In what other way can the critical function of staffing be carried out with professional effectiveness? In the management and use of administrative time, attention must be given to crucial and long-range concerns as well as to immediate day-to-day operational deadlines. Breaking up old, comfortable patterns is apt to be unsettling and painful, but it is often necessary for significant growth and improvement.

Implications for Adult and Continuing Education

The full impact of the involvement of adults in the educational scene will out of necessity be felt throughout the educational enterprise. The preceding chapters make clear that: organizational change and flexibility is essential, administering a continuing education program is complex, staff development is needed for teachers of adults, and additional research data are needed.

Organizational Change and Flexibility

The commitment of an organization to provide continuing education involves more than the provision of a new program. As the authors of the previous chapters have pointed out, the adult student can bring a whole new dimension to the organization. This is especially so for schools and universities as providers of continuing education.

Adult students come to the educational experience with a different frame of reference than traditional students. Not only do they have a more definite set of expectations but they also have experiences to bring to the class. For most adult students, education is not their primary endeavor; their jobs and families come first.

Most educational experiences for adults are not provided at the same time of day or on the same schedule as the usual educational offerings. An organization serving adult students will find it necessary to have counselors available in the late afternoon or evening, extended registration times, and modifications in library hours. Other student services will need to be altered to fit the time schedules of adult students.

With the addition of faculty members who work part-time or full-time there needs to be a conscious effort to have secretarial support, duplication services, audiovisual services, and other faculty support services available when needed. Furthermore, regular activites such as faculty meetings, committee assignments, and preparation for tenure and promotion decisions often do not fit the schedule of teachers who work with adults. If arrangements are not adjusted, faculty members will find themselves working extra hours simply because they are teaching adults. Low faculty morale could become a problem.

The result is the need for ongoing organizational change. This may not be significant in cost, but it will mean adjustment of the traditional patterns of operation followed by administrator, faculty member, and support staff.

It is easy to assume that once organizations have changed to accommodate adults, no further changes will be necessary. This is not so. If organizations are to serve adult clientele, they must be flexible and continually adapt. Eligibility requirements for certain courses, attendance patterns, and time to complete work will not be likely to fit the needs of every adult. The illness of a family member, a job transfer, a new assignment, the birth of a child or any of a number of life problems will change previously established rules. Program flexibility is the key to successfully helping adults in their educational endeavors.

Complexity of Administration

The experiences of administrators demonstrate that the process of administering a continuing education program is complex and unique.

While the administrators of traditional school programs can rely on continuous support, the administrator of a continuing education program must frequently conduct courses on a self-supporting basis. Until registration is complete, it is not known whether a particular course will be offered. The ambiguity of the situation creates complex problems for administrators.

The part-time teaching staff is another unique feature. The administrator of the traditional school program has a permanent cadre of faculty to teach courses, whereas the continuing education administrator hires teachers each term based on the needs of a changing clientele.

Numerous other illustrations could be given to show the unique situations faced by administrators of continuing education programs. The complexity of the educational program requires administrators with special capabilities.

Need for Staff Development. The need for faculty development has been carefully documented and illustrated in previous chapters. Faculty members are not the only ones in a continuing education agency who need staff development to work effectively with adult learners.

Administrators and support staff (secretaries, registration personnel, library staff, security personnel, counselors, and others) also need help in understanding adult participants. First, there is a need to recognize that adults who have been away from school for some time may not understand the terminology used in the organization. In educational institutions such terms as line schedule, drop-add form, late drop, and permit to register may not be familiar. Just helping support staff members understand that they need to explain organizational jargon will help some adults adjust to new educational experiences.

Administrators also need to know about the special needs and characteristics of adult learners so that staff members can be helped to work effectively with them. It is easy to forget that all students are not alike.

Research Needed. Several authors have cited a need for research on working with adult students. Some have applied theories and research findings from the behavioral sciences to the teaching of adults. The adult student phenomenon and a career path for teachers of adults are relatively new to many people. As a result, continuing educators and others are just beginning to develop a solid research base.

Two tasks should be accomplished. First, teachers and administrators who work with adult students should identify the pressing research questions. Second, continuing educators should catalog and disseminate research generalizations that are presently available. This sourcebook is a beginning for the latter task.

Summary

This sourcebook has described the state of the art related to the recruitment, selection, development, supervision, and recognition of teachers of adults. Recognizing the importance of the staffing function and noting the gap between what is being done and what can be done leads to the conclusion that continuing education administrators should be committed to improving their staffing practices. With the rapidly increasing numbers of adults in continuing education and the increased emphasis on improving program quality, our present staffing practices may soon become obsolete. This sourcebook is a useful guide for working with teachers of adults as we enter the 1980s.

References

Cross, K. P. "Adult Learners: Characteristics, Needs, and Interests." In R. E. Peterson and Associates (Eds.), *Lifelong Learning in America: An Overview of Current Practices, Available Resources, and Future Prospects*. San Francisco: Jossey-Bass, 1979.

Jerry Parsons is currently professor of adult and continuing education at Kansas State University. In 1980 he will become state leader of 4-H and youth programs with the university extension service, Iowa State University.

Continuing education administrators can purchase, borrow, or rent audiovisual resources that will help implement a staffing strategy.

Supplementary Audiovisual Resources

Darlene W. Elberling

The foregoing chapters in this sourcebook provide useful concepts and examples regarding the staffing process. These chapters and their references can help practitioners increase their understanding of staffing. In this chapter I will identify alternative supplementary audiovisual resources that could serve as an alternative to reading.

Continuing education administrators who prefer to increase their proficiency by the use of films and videotapes might do so in any of several ways. One would be for a practitioner to order and view a film or tape and use any helpful ideas that might result. Another way (for larger continuing education agencies) would be for a number of staff members to review the audiovisual resources and discuss the implications for staffing. These resources could also be used in meetings of associations of continuing education administrators at local, state, regional, and national levels.

The use of audiovisual materials can add a dimension of creativity and dynamism in implementing the staffing process. It is an alternative that can stimulate thought and discussion—providing a vicarious experiential activity to enhance other learning. Numerous audiovisual teaching aids are available for both administrators and teachers of adults. Although less portable than the print medium, audiovisual aids have appeal as alternative modes for acquiring information and skills. They may be preferred by individuals who learn more successfully or rapidly through audio or visual senses. They may also appeal as educational tools because they contain a degree of entertainment or novelty value.

Formats and Selection

The commonly used types or formats of audiovisual aids (or software) include 16mm films, videocassettes, and audiocassettes. Although slides, filmstrips, and 8mm films on instructional topics do exist, they are not as accessible or as frequently produced commercially. The selection of an appropriate format depends on several factors.

Intended Audience. How many persons will be involved, and do they have any special needs or preferences? Video- and audiocassettes are most effectively used by individuals or by small groups. 16mm films can be an individual experience, but are typically directed to a larger group.

Setting. What is the size of the room? Is the site stationary or a moving vehicle? And what is the room-darkening capability? Audiocassettes can be very practical in both stationary or moving vehicle situations. Videocassette players can easily be seen in dimmed or natural light. Film requires significant darkening of the viewing area.

Content. What is the importance of motion or size of the image to maximum communication? Some concepts can be adequately expressed through sound alone; others require visual treatment. The effect of a large or small screen can be a deciding factor.

Accessibility

Audiovisual aids can be purchased, rented, or borrowed.

Purchasing. A selected list of distributors and producers can be found at the end of this chapter. Certain distributors tend to specialize in management or instructional topics, and their catalogues are readily available. Such catalogues can be useful as tools for both planning and purchase. Most distributors will forward material for preview on request.

Renting. University film services are a good source of rental materials. Holdings are usually extensive and catalogues of the collection are arranged by subject and title, with codes indicating distributor. Entries usually include a brief annotation, the year of production, running time, format, and (where applicable) color or black-and-white designation.

Borrowing. Public libraries—whether municipal, regional, county or network—frequently maintain film collections. These collections vary in size and breadth of subject, and a small fee may be charged. Videocassettes may be found in some libraries; audiocassettes are usually found in appropriate subject areas or departments.

Content Evaluation and Selection

Several national journals regularly review audiovisual materials. Examples of these journals include *Previews* (published by R. R. Bowker), *Film News, Film Library Quarterly,* and *Sightlines.* Reviews can be valuable in selecting a list of recommended titles for possible review—or as the authority when personal preview is impractical. Public and academic librarians can be good resources, and public school media specialists have considerable expertise in audiovisual selection. Bibliographies can be located through ERIC Clearinghouses.

A Sample List

The following list is a sample of current titles that are related to the staffing functions discussed in this sourcebook. No qualitative recommendations are implied. Although titles are arranged by subject, many could easily be listed under more than one designation. The superscript number following each citation corresponds to the list of distributors at the end of the chapter.

Recruitment and Selection.
The Face-to-Face Payoff: Dynamics of the Interview (16mm film, color, 30 min.)[6] Shows how administrators can improve interviewing skills and demonstrates techniques.
The Making of a Decision (16mm film, b/w and color, 32 min., c.1973)[11] Demonstrates a rational decision-making process for supervisors and deals specifically with the problem of selection for promotion.
The Uncalculated Risk (16mm film, color, 26 min., c.1973)[11] Helps in distinguishing inference from observation in personnel decisions.
Women in Business: Threat or Opportunity? (16mm film, color, 30 min., 1975)[4] Explores stereotypes, addresses issues and roles developing from affirmative action programs, and discusses the opportunities available to meet the challenge.

Supervision.
A Case of Insubordination (16mm film, b/w and color, 20 min., c.1973)[11] Presents case studies in perception, communications, and handling conflicts, and shows one incident as perceived by an employee, a supervisor, a witness, and an arbitrator.
Overcoming Resistance to Change (16mm film, b/w and color, 30 min., c.1973)[11] Shows how to recognize the emotional factors that breed resistance to change and gives suggestions on how to prevent and overcome resistance.
Is It All Over? The Termination Interview (16mm film, color, 6 min.)[6] Shows how this interview can become a learning and building experience for the employee.

Productivity and the Self-Fulfilling Prophecy: The Pygmalion Effect (16mm film, color, 30 min., 1975)[4] Shows how the powers of expectation can be used to influence positively or negatively; features Rensis Likert and Douglas McGregor.

Effective Organization Series (16mm films, color, 30 min. each, 1971)[2] The six films are *Assessing Management Potential, Management by Participation, Pay for Performance, Making Human Resources Productive, Team Building,* and *Confronting Conflict.* Features Saul Gellerman.

The "How To" Drucker—A Practicing Manager's Day-to-Day Guide (4 audiocassettes, booklet)[1] Presents Peter Drucker in interview format and discusses the important aspects of managerial performance.

Listening (16mm film, color, 14 min., c.1973)[11] Demonstrates the importance of good listening habits.

The Man in the Middle (16mm film, b/w, 28 min., c.1973)[11] Shows supervisors the complexity of supervisory positions and the benefits of supervisory training.

Mastering the Art of Delegating (audiocassette no. 5 in the series "Executive Seminars in Sound")[5] Other cassettes in the series address time management, organization, getting ideas across, people management, and strategies for moving ahead.

The Mature Executive (3 audiocassettes, booklet)[1] Discusses the mature executive in terms of wisdom, experience, positive attitude toward change, enthusiasm, and a receptivity to the ideas of others.

Problem Solving—Some Basic Principles (16mm film, color, 18 min., c.1973)[11] Presents a systematic approach to problem solving and decision making.

The Way I See It (16mm film, b/w and color, 23 min, c.1973)[11] Shows what can happen when goals are not set, objectives are not clearly defined, and review points are not established.

Berlo Communication (16mm films, color, 24 min. each, 1965)[2] Includes five titles: *Avoiding Communication Breakdown, Meanings Are in People, Communication Feedback, Changing Attitudes Through Communication,* and *Communicating Management's Point of View.*

A Measure of Understanding (16mm film, b/w and color, 29 min., c.1973)[11] Focuses on the problems involved in communicating meaning, attitudes, and intentions.

Person to Person Communication (16mm film, b/w and color, 14 min., c.1973)[11] Stresses awareness of the unspoken factors that affect communication: assumptions, viewpoints, feelings.

Staff Development.

Welcome Aboard (16mm film, color, 21 min., c.1973)[11] Discusses employee orientation.

Career Development: A Plan for All Seasons (16mm film, color, 26 min., 1978)[9] Describes the philosophy behind analyzing an employee's work goals and coordinating them with the organization's plans for positive, directed results.
Getting Ahead: The Road to Self-Development (16mm film, b/w and color, 28 min., c.1973)[11] Encourages self-evaluation, target setting, and continuing education among employees.
Imagination at Work (16mm film, b/w and color, 21 min., c.1973)[11] Shows the techniques and skills of creative thinking with suggestions for their application: sensitivity, fluency, flexibility, and originality.
Meeting in Progress (16mm film, color, 43 min., c.1973)[11] Provides a means of teaching conference leadership through group participation.
Can Adults Learn? (Videocassette from series "Basic Education: Teaching the Adult," color, 30 min., 1975)[8] Discusses adult learning capabilities and physiological changes. Series includes 30 half-hour videocassettes.
Conversations with Doers—Not Doubters (audiocassette series—12 cassettes)[7] Discusses the important aspects of the world-wide technology movement in education and training today.
Development and Management of Instructional Systems (3 videocassette programs, color, print materials available, sound/slide available, 40 sequenced hours)[10] Presents basic understanding of instructional system design and development—part group-paced and part self-paced.
Rewards and Incentives.
Almost Everything You Wanted to Know About Motivating People, or Maslow's Hierarchy of Needs (16mm film, color, guide, 15 min., 1975)[12] Explores Maslow's theory and the area of human motivation as applicable to work situations.
Motivation and Personality (series of 6 audiocassettes, supplements 16mm film series with same titles, 28 min. per title, also available in ¾ inch videocassette)[2] Includes *Understanding Motivation, Motivation Through Job Achievement, The Self-Motivated Achiever, Human Nature and Organizational Realities, The Management of Human Assets,* and *Theory X and Y: Parts I and II* (the work of Douglas McGregor).
Motivation and Productivity (series of 9 16mm films, color, guide, 20–28 min., 1967–1969)[2] Film series coordinates with *Motivation and Personality* audiocassettes.
Motivation to Work (series of 5 16mm films, color, guide, 21–25 min., 1969)[2] Includes *Modern Meaning of Efficiency, Kita, or What Have You Done for Me Lately?, Job Enrichment in Action, Building a Climate for Individual Growth,* and *The ABC Man: the Manager in Mid-Career.* Explores Herzberg's theories of motivation.
Evaluation.
How Supervisors Should Appraise Employee Performance (16mm film, color, 23 min., 1979)[3] Shows how to conduct appraisals to reduce turnover,

discover talent, and uncover employee discontent; includes real-life dramatizations.

Judging People (16mm film, b/w, 23 min., c.1973)[11] Teaches practical techniques of appraising performance, assigning work, and delegating.

Performance and Potential Review (16mm film, from series, "Management by Objectives," color, 21 min., 1969)[2] Illustrates measurement of performance results against objectives.

Performance Appraisal: The Human Dynamics (16mm film, color, 25 min., 1978)[9] Illustrates the mutual exchange of ideas as a preferred method of performance appraisal.

You're Coming Along Fine (16mm film, b/w and color, 23 min., c.1973)[11] Shows the importance of establishing mutually shared objectives and giving honest feedback; case study.

Distributors

1. AMACOM, American Management Association, 135 W. 50th St., New York, NY 10020.
2. BNA Communications, Inc., 9401 Decoverly Hall Road, Rockville, MD 20850.
3. Bureau of Business Practice, 24 Rope Ferry Rd., Waterford, CT 06386.
4. CRM Educational Films, 110 15th St., Delmar, CA 92014.
5. Chamber of Commerce of the United States, 1615 H St. N.W., Washington, D.C. 20062.
6. Creative Media, 820 Keo Way, Des Moines, IA 50309.
7. Educational Technology Magazine, 140 Sylvan Ave., Englewood Cliffs, NJ 37632.
8. Maryland State Department of Education, Division of Instructional Television, P.O. Box 8717, Baltimore-Washington International Airport, Baltimore, MD 21240.
9. McGraw-Hill Textfilms, 512 Burlington Ave., LaGrange, IL 60525.
10. The National Laboratory for the Advancement of Education, Aerospace Education Foundation, 1750 Pennsylvania Ave. N.W., Washington, D.C. 20006.
11. Roundtable Films, Inc., 113 N. San Vincente Blvd., Beverly Hills, CA 90211.
12. Salenger Educational Media, 1635 12th St., Santa Monica, CA 90404.

Darlene W. Elberling is a community librarian with the Minneapolis Public Library and Information Center. She is completing her doctorate in adult education at the University of Minnesota.

Index

A

Administration, complexity of, 85-86
Administrators: evaluation by, 73-74; leadership by, 51-52; philosophy of, 3, 16; planning by, 28-29; support by, 51-53
Aker, G. F., 7, 14
AMACOM, 94
American Federation of Teachers, 57
American Society for Training and Development, 7
Anderson, T., 61, 70
Andragogy: or conditioning, 42-43; theory of, 4, 30
Applications, processing of, 13
Arceri, J. M., 43, 49
Argyris, C., 51, 58

B

Bergevin, P., 31, 37
Bessent, W., 26, 37
Bezdek, W. E., 17, 24
Blanchard, K. H., 42, 49
Blaney, J., 16, 24
BNA Communications, Inc., 94
Bock, L., 61, 70
Booth, A., 5, 14
Boshier, R. W., 17, 24
Bruny, S. P., 73, 78
Bureau of Business Practice, 94
Burgess, P., 17, 24
Burkhart, R. C., 73, 74, 79
Burrichter, A. W., 40, 49

C

Campbell, R. F., 40, 49
Central value positions, 41-42
Chamber of Commerce of the United States, 94
Classrooms, management of, 28, 43-44
Collective bargaining, 57-58
Continuing education: barriers to improvement of, 82; challenges to, 82-84; change and flexibility in, 85; conceptual framework for, 5; content or process in, 4-5
Corbally, J. E., Jr., 40, 49
Courses: content of, and selection, 16-17; developing, 31-32; evaluation of, 32-33
Craig, R. L., 7, 14, 30, 37
Creative Media, 94
CRM Educational Films, 94
Cross, K. P., 17, 24, 81, 87

D

Daigneault, G. H., 8, 14
Dale, E., 31, 37
Davis, L. N., 36, 37
Davison, C. V., 73, 79
Development, staff: analysis of, 25-38; audiovisual resources for, 92-93; defined, ix, 26; in-service education as, 29-35; models for, 35-37; orientation as, 26-29; rationale for, 25-26, 86; and support, 57
Dissatisfaction, avoiding, 52-56, 67-68
Doyle, K. D., Jr., 73, 79

E

Eble, K. E., 73, 79
Educational Orientation Questionnaire, 19, 20
Educational Resources Information Center (ERIC), 8, 91
Educational Technology Magazine, 94
Eisner, E. W., 77-78, 79
Evaluation: by administrators, 73-74; analysis of, 71-79; audiovisual resources for, 93-94; of courses, 32-33; defined, ix, 72; formative and summative, 72; issues in, 83-84; learning as criterion in, 74-78; of recruitment, 13; strategies for, 72-

95

Evaluation (continued)
75; by students, 73; and supervision, 44-45

F

Fenn, N. E., Jr., 73, 79
Fisk, M., 7, 14
Florida Atlantic University, 46, 49n

G

Gage, N. L., 73, 79
Gale Research Company, 7
Gardner, D. L., 40, 49
Gowin, D. B., 8, 14
Grabowski, S. M., 8, 14, 62, 70

H

Hadley, H. N., 19, 24
Haimann, T., 40, 49
Hanna, E., 60, 61, 70
Hansen, G. L., 62, 70
Harris, B. M., 26, 37, 43, 49
Havighurst, R. J., 30, 37
Hersey, P., 42, 49
Herzberg, F., ix, x, 41, 49, 51-52, 54, 56, 58, 61, 70, 93
Hildebrand, M., 73, 79
Hilgert, F. L., 40, 49
Holt, E. B., 42, 49
Houle, C.O., viii, x, 17, 24, 35-36, 37

I

Illinois, University of, Urbana, 63, 64
Ingalls, J. D., 36, 37, 43, 49
In-service education: advisory committees for, 33-34; goals of, 29; policy issues of, 34-35; and supervision, 46, 47-49
Institutions: goals and structure of, 26-27; mission of, 16, 64; policies and rules of, 27-28, 30
Interview, for selection, 20-23

J

Jelinek, J. J., 41-42, 43, 49
Job description, and recruitment, 3-4

K

Kempfer, H., 4, 14
Kidd, J. R., 7, 14, 30, 37
Kinkaid, H. V., 62, 70
Klink, A. L., 62, 70
Knowles, M. S., 4, 14, 30, 36, 37, 43, 49, 73, 79
Knox, A. B., viii, x, 30, 35, 37, 60, 70
Kozoll, C. E., 61, 70
Kramer, R. E., 62, 70
Kubie, L. S., 40-41, 49

L

Learning, as evaluation criterion, 74-78
Levinson, D. J., 30, 37
Listening, in interview, 21-22
Lockheed Missile and Space Co., DIALOG service of, 7
Lorber, M. A., 75, 79
Luke, R., 35, 37

M

McCallon, E., 36, 37
McGraw-Hill Textfilms, 94
McGregor, D., 41, 49, 51, 58, 92, 93
McNeil, J. D., 74, 79
Mager, R. F., 31, 37, 76, 79
Maryland State Department of Education, 94
Maslow, A. H., 41, 49, 51, 58, 60, 70, 93
Mausner, B., 41, 49
Medsker, L., 61, 70
Merriam, S., 30, 38
Messerschmidt, D. H., 62, 70
Miller, L., 30, 38
Mocker, D. W., 62, 70
Moffett, G. M., 74, 79
Morris, D. M., 31, 37
Motivations, of teachers, 40-42, 56-57, 59, 60-63
Motivator-hygiene theory, ix, 41, 51-52, 61-62

N

National Education Association, 34
National Laboratory for the Advancement of Education, 94

National University Extension Association, 65
Needs: assessment of, 46, 47-49; hierarchy of, 41, 60
Niemi, J. A., 73, 79

O

Objectives, instructional, 31, 74, 76, 77-78
Observation, and selection, 19
Orientation: and administrative support, 52-53; as staff development, 26-29

P

Park, R. J., viii, x, 62, 70
Patton, C. V., 60, 70
Pierce, W. D., 75, 79
Principles of Adult Learning Scale (PALS), 19-20
Publications, as recruitment sources, 6-9

R

Ramseyer, J. A., 40, 49
Rauch, D. B., 40, 50
Recruitment: analysis of, 1-14; audiovisual resources for, 91; basis of, 1-2; defined, viii; evaluation of, 13; methods for, 12; notices for, 13; plan for, 11-13; schedule for, 12-13; specifications for, 3-5, 11, 21
References, and selection, 19
Rewards: analysis of, 59-70; audiovisual resources for, 93; communicating, 68-69; defined, ix; extrinsic, 60, 63-65; intrinsic, 60-61, 65-67; motivation related to, 63-68; and support, 54-56, 57, 65
Rink, D. L., 62, 70
Rosenberg, L., 17, 24
Roundtable Films, Inc., 94

S

Salenger Educational Media, 94
Scriven, M., 72, 79
Selection: aids in, 18-20; analysis of, 15-24; audiovisual resources for, 91; defined, viii-ix, 15; and educational environment, 16-18; and government guidelines, 17-18; and search committee, 18-19, 83; written instruments for, 19-20
Sergiovanni, T. J., 56, 58
Shaw, N. C., 40, 50
Sheehy, G., 30, 38
Sheldon, J. A., 1, 14
Skinner, B. F., 43, 50
Smith, R. L., 73, 79
Smith, R. M., 7, 14, 16, 24, 31, 37
Smithsonian Scientific Information Exchange (SSIE), 8
Solomon, D., 17, 24
Staff development. *See* Development, staff
Staffing: audiovisual resources for, 89-94; functions in, viii-x; future of, 81-87; perspectives on, vii-x; priority of, vii-viii; status of, vii
Stake, R. E., 72, 79
Stanton, S., 2, 14
Strother, G. B., 60, 70
Students, adult: centrality of, 81-82; characteristics of, 4, 17, 30; evaluation by, 73; retention and recruitment of, 45-46
Supervision: of adult teachers, 39-40; analysis of, 39-50; applications for, 43-47; audiovisual resources for, 91-92; defined, ix, 40; role of, 40; and support, 54
Support, administrative, ix, 51-58
Snydermann, B., 41, 49
System Development Corporation, ORBIT service of, 7

T

Targeted evaluation approach (TEA), 75-78
Tarvin, L., 61, 70
Teachers: characteristics of, 2-3, 4, 15; motivations of, 40-42, 56-57, 59, 60-63; part-time, issue of, 83; pay policies for, 55; sources of, 5-10, 11-12; working conditions for, 53-54
Teaching: aids for, 31, 46-47; techniques of, 30-31, 44
Theory X-Theory Y, 41
Tyler, R. W., 72, 74, 79

U

Ulmer, C., 35, 37, 62, 70

V

Van Dersal, W. R., 40, 41, 42, 50
Verner, C., 5, 14

W

Wasinger, G. B., 1, 14
Watkins, B., 57, 58
Whipple, J. B., 4, 5, 14
Wilson, L. C., 39, 50
Wilson, R. C., 73, 79

Z

Zinn, L. M., 62, 70